CATHERINE LIM

Romancing the Language

CATHERINE LIM
Romancing the Language
A Writer's Lasting Love Affair with English

Cover design by Benson Tan
Cover image of typewriter created by Kues1 - Freepik.com

Published by Marshall Cavendish Editions
An imprint of Marshall Cavendish International

A member of the
Times Publishing Group

Other Marshall Cavendish Offices: Marshall Cavendish Corporation. 99 White Plains Road, Tarrytown NY 10591-9001, USA • Marshall Cavendish International (Thailand) Co Ltd. 253 Asoke, 12th Flr, Sukhumvit 21 Road, Klongtoey Nua, Wattana, Bangkok 10110, Thailand • Marshall Cavendish (Malaysia) Sdn Bhd, Times Subang, Lot 46, Subang Hi-Tech Industrial Park, Batu Tiga, 40000 Shah Alam, Selangor Darul Ehsan, Malaysia

Marshall Cavendish is a registered trademark of Times Publishing Limited

National Library Board, Singapore Cataloguing-in-Publication Data

Name(s): Lim, Catherine.
Title: Romancing the language : a writer's lasting love affair with English / Catherine Lim.
Description: Singapore : Marshall Cavendish Editions, [2018]
Identifier(s): OCN 1034688147 I ISBN 978-981-48-2814-7 (paperback)
Subject(s): LCSH: Lim, Catherine--Anecdotes. I Authors, Singaporean--Ancedotes. I English language--Ancedotes. I English language--Humor.
Classification: DDC S823--dc23

Printed in Singapore

CONTENTS

Mother Tongue

It's said that even if you speak several languages, there's only one in which you live — your mother tongue.

The language in which I live, breathe, think and dream is, by that definition, not the Hokkien of my parents and their parents, and their parents' parents, all the way back to the southern Chinese province of Fukien, where we came from, so long ago. It is English. English is my mother tongue in the fullest, most meaningful sense of the word. I started speaking it only when I was already six, well past that narrow window of time during which, according to the psychologists, children pick up any language they hear and speak it fluently, effortlessly.

Mother tongue. That name is far more appealing than its prosaic synonyms of 'native language' or 'first language'. For it has a resonance all its own, with its powerful combination of two primordial images that evoke strong emotion — the first, at the individual level, of the biology of birth and bonding; and the second, at the highest level of the human species, the evolutionary development of language, over thousands of years, that has made our species unique on the face of the planet.

The two images come together, movingly, in the universal language of motherese, the first speech sounds that a baby hears from its mother, as their faces are drawn close together in smiling wonderment, establishing a permanent link between language, need and identity, in whatever diverse paths the combined interactions of these three forces will take throughout the individual's life. The importance of motherese must have been the impetus behind UNESCO's establishment of International Mother Language Day which takes place on 21 February.

There could have been something of the emotional impact of motherese in my first contact with English when I attended a convent school at the age of six, in the little town of Kulim in the north of peninsular Malaysia, then called Malaya. The sheer excitement of the new language had instantly relegated the Hokkien of my birth and upbringing to secondary position. It seemed that I was walking into a brave new world. By about the age of ten, I had not only learnt to speak the language of the colonial masters fluently, but had become fully aware of its political and socio-economic power that my native Hokkien could never aspire to.

This awareness had made me, alas, even at that age, a most unlikeable snob and prig whose behaviour, in today's open-minded, eclectic and egalitarian society, would be roundly — and justifiably — censured on social media. The self-consciousness had actually led me to conduct a secret research on many of my schoolmates, mainly during the school recess which lasted about twenty minutes when we could talk freely in the school playground. My sense of social superiority made me see an unmistakable correlation between their parents' low social status and the absence of an English education. Their fathers were mainly labourers, rubber tappers, peons, coffeeshop attendants, hawkers, lorry drivers, poultry or fish sellers in the town's only market, ticket sellers or attendants in the town's only cinema, shopkeepers, managers of small family businesses, then later perhaps owners themselves of small businesses such as the laundry or groceries business, on an excruciatingly slow ascent in the claim to prosperity and social status.

One classmate never wanted it to be known that her father was a trishaw pedaller. Every morning he sent her to school in his trishaw before he pedalled off to earn his living taking other schoolchildren to their schools. One day, when she had forgotten to take her pocket money from him to buy the usual rice bun to eat during the school recess, he called after her loudly, in the full view and hearing of her classmates, and she turned, red-faced with shame and anger, to walk back slowly and pick up the small coin from his outstretched palm.

It would only be much later that I realised that a more worthwhile subject of study, for which socio-economic status was not at all relevant, was human relationship itself, and its basis in human nature. I wanted to explore in depth the relationships between parents and children, husbands and wives, men and women, the rich and the poor, in all their complexities, conflicts and subtle ironies. But as a schoolgirl, I could only feel the pain and embarrassment of my classmate whose father never went to school, much less an English school, and had to support his family through one of the humblest forms of livelihood, on a par with road-sweeping and garbage collecting.

My own father had a reasonable English education that enabled him to earn a living as an accountant. English was not his mother tongue, as it was mine. But he spoke it fluently enough, although his education in English fell far short of the kind that was necessary to pave the way towards a social standing and elitism, which could hope to match, but even then only remotely, that enjoyed by the British community. These lived in exclusive bungalows with large gardens and did their shopping at Robinson's in Penang, rather than at the modest stores in Kulim. The kind of education that dared aspire to this lifestyle had to be of the advanced type, indeed, so advanced as to be beyond the reach of the majority.

For a start, it necessitated going through several stages of the educational system, which was based strictly on the British model. Each stage was more demanding than the preceding one, so that by the end of the whole process, none of the cohorts from the beginning would be left. All would have fallen by the plebeian wayside. It was like an arduous ascent to a mountain peak that remained haughtily beyond reach.

The strenuous educational system started with primary education lasting six years. Halfway through, a number from my Primary One cohort had left, for a variety of reasons: inability to continue paying the monthly school fees and other school expenses, the necessity to stay home to do the housework in place of the mother who had once again given birth, the need to help out at the father's noodles stall in the market, or simply the need to drop out of an education based on a foreign language that was just too difficult to learn. One classmate left because of illness brought on by malnutrition; another, aged twelve, was asked to leave because the nuns suspected she was pregnant.

The secondary school phase, lasting four years, saw more dwindling of numbers. Several of my classmates left to take up jobs as waitresses or to get married. If we managed to make it through secondary school, our education culminated in the taking of the all-important General Certificate of Education examination, administered by the University of Cambridge, where the exam papers were sent to be marked and graded. By that time, candidates would have been sixteen or seventeen years old, and poised to take their place in the working world.

The Cambridge Certificate was invaluable as a means, in a certificate-conscious society, to get any job that required the ability to speak and read in English, such as in a post office or a bank. Such jobs were few and were won only after strong competition. Getting a good grade certified by the Cambridge Examinations Syndicate greatly improved the candidate's chances. It was, moreover, rewarded by much family pride and congratulatory good wishes from neighbours.

There was a girl in our town, several years my senior, who, when she found out that she had failed in the exam, locked herself in her room and committed suicide by repeatedly stabbing her throat with a pair of scissors. Her grieving parents took the trouble of getting an English-educated neighbour to fake a Cambridge Certificate, meticulously copied from a real one, to place in the coffin with her.

Fortunately for me, my good grade in the Cambridge exam paved the way to the higher education I coveted. By this stage, I was the only one left of the original cohort to make it to university, supported all the way by modest scholarships and money earned from giving private tuition to Chinese-educated students who felt, perhaps with a twinge of resentment, that a working knowledge of the foreign language was necessary at some stage in their careers.

The highest point of an English education (which I never achieved) was its continuation and culmination in the birthplace of the language itself, that is, Great Britain. It was the dream and ambition of many to get into one of the prestigious colleges or universities there, and return home with even more burnished certificates, diplomas or degrees. The ultimate desire, buried deep in the Malaysian psyche, was to get a medical degree and come home with the prestigious appellation of 'Dr' attached to the name. A 'Dr Tan Oon Teik' or a 'Dr A.S. Sinnathamby' was, by virtue of that title, superior to a mere 'Mr James Williamson' or 'Mr Arthur McCullough'.

If the ambitious young doctor, returning to his hometown, soon set up his own clinic, his proud parents could die happy. I remember a man who insisted that his son's name on the sign plate outside his clinic was not conspicuous enough. He wanted the 'DR' to be stretched out to a full 'DOCTOR', spelt out in bold capital letters. One day he got very annoyed with a Malay *mee rebus* seller who had parked his large cart outside the clinic, not only blocking sight of the sign plate, but degrading it by close proximity to the rickety cart piled with cheap-looking yellow noodles and vegetables. The man angrily waved the offender away with a string of English expletives he had picked up from his son.

I also remember a neighbour, a middle-aged woman who never referred to her son, a graduate from a medical college in Scotland, other than as *lo koon* which was Hokkien for 'doctor'. The maidservant was told precisely and frequently that *lo koon* wanted to eat this or that, that *lo koon* didn't like his shirts starched too much. One day the maidservant absentmindedly put one of the doctor's shirts in the large family washtub in which there was already a pile of used female undergarments, thereby violating the tradition that strictly forbade such close contact and contamination. She was severely scolded by the mistress of the house. "Don't you dare do that again. Do you want to bring bad luck to *lo koon*?" His name had become forever submerged by the honorific.

The medical profession was the crème de la crème in society. The few doctors in Kulim drove along the town's one main road, in a Ford or Morris Minor, alongside bicycles, trishaws and the occasional bullock cart. They ate in the best local restaurants and never in the open-air food stalls in the marketplace, where sometimes the rickshaw pedaller, who kept his place at the bottom of the totem pole, squatted barefoot on a bench, and finished his bowl of steaming boiled rice in seconds, shovelling it into his mouth with chopsticks that moved so fast you saw only a blur. The doctors were not necessarily disdainful of the crude, simple folk but said they really enjoyed the steaks, sausages and pork chops in the one or two restaurants specially set up to cater to the British community nostalgic for home food, and with plenty of money to spend for it.

Dr Thong, one of my father's friends, regularly dined at a restaurant reputed to provide the best western food in town. It was originally called 'Lock Kee Restaurant', but the good doctor had persuaded the owner, Ah Bah, to change the name to 'Lucky Restaurant'. Ah Bah, whose English was limited to polite greetings, salutations and apologies of "Goo eev-vening, Lok-tor Thong", "Goo bye, Meester and Meesus Lobinson", "Tank you velly much", "Sol-ee, pe-lease execute me, my Eeng-lis not so good", was amiable enough, moreover, to allow the doctor to commemorate a great British royal event by changing the name of his wife's family business from 'Chia Soon Coffee Shop' to 'Coronation Place'.

As the ultimate gesture of benign patronage, Dr Thong told Ah Bah that from henceforth he would call him 'Johnny'. Ah Bah laughed loudly and good-naturedly, revealing a full set of gold teeth that he was secretly determined to keep, despite the doctor advising him, with a sad shake of the head, to replace with proper teeth, as gold teeth had long since lost their value as a status symbol.

Once Dr Thong invited a British couple he had gotten to know, a Mr and Mrs Graham, to dine with him at the Lucky Restaurant. As they ate and laughed heartily, a little group of the town's urchins clustered at the doorway to look at the sumptuous-looking pork chops, covered thickly with gravy and surrounded by luscious potatoes and green peas, that Ah Bah had expertly cooked and was now placing in front of his guests. The urchins, young boys with dirty bare feet and wearing only rough black cotton trousers held up with string, stared, gaped and gawked at the exotic fare, scratching their backs and armpits where the mosquitoes had bitten. The aroma of the good stuff emboldened them to take deep breaths and make excited comments to each other. Dr Thong said, with a great show of annoyance, "Johnny, please shoo them away. How can we eat properly with them staring like that!" Ah Bah rushed at them, shouting some dialect curses, and they fled. "The riff-raff of the town," said the doctor apologetically to his guests.

In one of my stories years later, set in Singapore, the protagonist is a Dr John Thong who speaks impeccable Queen's English. But his wife (whom he was obliged to marry because her businessman father had financed his medical studies in the UK) speaks a bad, ungrammatical local variety called Singlish. He is thoroughly ashamed when she speaks loudly and cheerfully at the classy formal functions to which men are expected to bring their wives. Back home, he vents his irritation:

"Why must you keep talking endlessly? Weren't you in the least bit aware that Mrs Ramachandran wasn't at all interested?"

"Why? Cannot talk at party — uh? So what to do? Eat and eat. Get more and more fat, uh? The food this time not so good, I tell you. I tell Mrs Lamachanlan, and she agree. Prawns — aiyah — not porperly cook, I tell you!"

"Could I ask you urgently to refrain in future from raising your voice and laughing so loudly? There are important, respectable people around. And don't gossip so much. It's not at all becoming of a woman with a husband who commands no small respect in society."

"Aiyah, lespect, what lespect. What gossip? I never gossip,

say bad thing about people. And what, cannot laugh at party,
meh? Everybody laugh, why you never kee-ticise them?"

"They talk and laugh like civilised people. You talk and
laugh like a fishwife. Do you know you are a source of great
embarrassment to me?"

"All-light, all-light! Next time you don't ask me go to any
party. You go, I don't go. If people ask, say your wife speak
low class Eng-lis, not your good high class Eng-lis. You know
what? People like better to listen to me. This Mrs Ludoff Car-
ventish — her name very hard to pornounce — she say she
enjoy listen to me. You so prr-oud and show-off. Nobody like
listen to you, see?"

Head over Heels

From a young age, I saw that the Chinese community in Kulim was split into two camps — the English-educated, English-speaking minority, on one side; and, on the other, the dialect-speaking majority who had never gone to an English school or had dropped out after a few years. The two groups, facing each other across an unbridgeable socio-economic chasm, could not have differed more in their names, speech, dress, behaviour, occupations, manners and sense of identity.

"Roland Chow — you mean that man over there, standing by the pillar? His name is Roland Chow?"

"Yes."

"No, it can't be! He's wearing a singlet and khaki shorts, and he's picking his teeth!"

"Yes, that's Roland."

"Listen, he's shouting in vulgar Teochew to someone across the road. You MUST be mistaken."

"No, I'm not."

"Does he know how to pronounce his own name? I bet he calls himself 'Loleng Chow'. What does he do, for goodness' sake?"

"He's a delivery man working for my uncle."

"I knew it. Somebody must have given him that name. Surely not his parents?"

"The pastor in his church."

"Loleng Chow is a Christian? I bet he cannot stop the old ancestor-worshipping habits. I bet he faithfully observes the Festival of the Hungry Ghosts, and contributes to environmental pollution with all that burning of ghost money."

It was clear to my precociously shrewd, unabashedly opportunistic young mind where I wanted to position myself. With the winner of course. With English, the gateway to wealth and the good life and social respect.

It would only be years later, when my creativity as a writer was beginning to stir for the first time, that I was aware of the real power of English. It was more than just instrumental. It was also something that inhered deeply in the language, something intrinsic. It was its amazing expressiveness, made possible by its rich vocabulary, its syntax, its figures of speech, its metaphors and symbolisms, its very sound system. Here was a language that would surely serve every need of the creative writer. I had found a winner.

I studied this potential literary ally further, to see how it could enable me to become the kind of writer I wanted to be. My literary ambition had preceded my writing ability by decades, and soon each was driving and reinforcing the other, through the singular motivation of the English language. Here was a language, associated with the famous stiff upper lip of its native speakers, and their penchant for cool understatement and calm sarcasm, that exactly matched my perception of the consummate writer. For with quiet, meticulous ruthlessness, I had been observing the world around me and planning to write about them with the lofty, grim and scathing honesty that I thought every serious writer should have. The satirical pen and the English language were made for each other.

I had entered an Ali Baba cave of linguistic and literary treasures.

It is said that the English are an eccentric race, with the eccentricity duplicated wholesale in their language. But for me, eccentricity could never be used in any derogatory sense. I was ready to defend it as the reflection of carefree independence, creativity, inventiveness, uniqueness, genius.

I had fallen head over heels in love with a foreign language that others in my community were indifferent to, had grudgingly learnt or positively hated. I embraced the English language fully, wanting to learn everything about it, to celebrate it and serve it, like the completely enamoured and enslaved lover. I suppose I would have done the same with German or French or Mandarin or Russian if it had been the first foreign language that I had been introduced to, in a process not unlike the powerful imprinting that takes place when young ducklings open their eyes for the first time, see the boots of the farmer attending to them, and instantly become attached to the muddy footwear, following them everywhere with a great deal of excited quacking. I was the most ardent and vocal follower of English.

As I delved into the language, I grew particularly fond of a special feature — its figures of speech. Its very large vocabulary of descriptive terms to denote objects in everyday life, and of affective terms to convey feelings in all their nuances, would have been enough for me. I had marvelled, for instance, at the large number of words available to me if I wanted to describe anger on a rising scale, from mild annoyance, irritation and pique through exasperation, vexation and indignation to rage, wrath, fury, apoplexy. Or if I wanted to describe love exhaustively, I could have recourse to the astonishing range of adjectives for its many different forms: passionate, lustful, Platonic, chivalrous, erotic, sensuous, cerebral, carnal, idealistic, bestial, concupiscent, agapeic.

But the language offered much more, taking the learner beyond the literal to the figurative, thus opening up a wonderland of communicative power. I took instantly to the three figures of speech used for making comparisons, since I was always making comparisons. The simile, the metaphor and the symbol occurred in a series of increasingly more abbreviated, focused and intense analogies: *Life is like a voyage. The voyage of life. The voyage. Her dreams were like the waste after a shipwreck. The shipwreck of her dreams. Shipwreck.*

Short story writers like to have very condensed, stark titles for their stories, such as 'Bed', 'Wall', 'Chameleon', 'The Blue Kite', 'The Bridge', 'Water', 'White Ribbon', probably because of this concentration of symbolic power.

I revelled in the personification, the hyperbole and the litotes, the onomatopeia and assonance, alliteration and prosody, the prolepsis and the ellipsis, the anaphora and the cataphora, the amphibology and the paraprosdokian. An embarrassment of riches. A true mark of plenitude and majesty. I let each word roll luxuriously on my tongue, making sure I could pronounce, define and spell it correctly. To do less would be unforgivable lèse-majesté.

There was one figure of speech for which I quickly developed a special affinity — the pun. The pun, by which the sounds and meanings of words could be cleverly manipulated and played around to give them new, unexpected, often humorous meanings, gave me a special pleasure. I played with words as other children played with toys. The pun tickled the childlike aspect of my personality. *Sofa. So far, so good. A housebound husband. A meow meow Christmas and a yappy yappy New Year to all our pets!*

I even did visual versions of the puns. I drew a picture of a man lying on his sofa after he has just been thrown out of his window. He has not yet hit the ground and he says happily while still in the air: "Sofa, so good." I read a joke about a particularly captivating pun, and did a cartoon drawing of it too. It showed a farmer looking at two bugs, one larger than the other, wondering which to kill first and finally saying, "Of course. I'll choose the lesser weevil."

I tried to create my own puns using Hokkien words. *Pak-thor* in Hokkien means to romance, to indulge in romantic overtures. I created the pun *pak-thology* as a humorous comment on the whole range of maladies that poor besotted lovers were subject to, including lunacy. *Tidak apa* in colloquial Malay, the local lingua franca, means having an attitude of carelessness and indifference.

Tidak-apathy was a deliciously apt and serendipitous coinage. I thought of a sentence that could combine my two creations, and came up with a rather cute hybrid: 'She concluded that he was incapable of real *pak-thology* because of his annoying *tidak-apathy*.' I was determined that when the time came for me to write my short stories, I would impress my Singapore readers by weaving a story around this attention-grabbing sentence with its unmistakable local flavour.

The special appeal of the pun for me was in the ease in remembering and storing it for later sharing with other pun-lovers. I remember saving up a whole range of frivolous, juvenile jokes to amuse fellow students, such as that one of the judge sitting in the dentist's chair and severely warning the dentist, "Swear that you will take out the tooth, the whole tooth and nothing but the tooth!" I thought it was hilarious. Such jokes were best shared verbally, gesturally, than in written form.

And there was the one about a woman who was putting on so much weight that she moaned her lack of will "to practise girth control". The pun immediately spawned another, about an unruly audience laughing and clapping non-stop, that was sternly told to practise some *mirth* control.

The best pun of all, I thought, was the one that was making the rounds at a time when Mr Lee Kuan Yew, Singapore's first prime minister, was supposedly making sure that his successor, Mr Goh Chok Tong, was there just to warm the seat for his son, Mr Lee Hsien Loong. Singapore's three most influential men in politics, locked in a tense triangle of power, had inspired someone, possibly a Catholic, to come up with a pun based on the Holy Trinity. When I first heard 'The Father, Son and Holy Goh' pun, I was most impressed and was convinced that there must be a lot of playful punsters around in a society often described as dour and humourless.

The lowest form of humour? I think the pun has the highest dividend of laughter.

Now laughter can come in various forms, from the utterly crude to the commendably refined. The pun provides for the entire range, from the ribald, thigh-slapping type all the way to the restrained, genteel variety. I wanted to savour the whole range, being convinced that if you have found a good thing, you must have all of it. *Pau ka liow* was blasé Hokkien advice to 'take the whole damn thing. So what.' Besides I had never outgrown the juvenile penchant for low jokes of the graphic kind favoured by the pun. So what if it was decried by that most influential and respected writer of the first English language dictionary, Dr Samuel Johnson, who was the first to call it the lowest form of humour.

"But," the convent nuns who taught me always to be ladylike would have gently remonstrated, "you needn't, you know, go for the coarse pun at all. Keep to the refined end", with a little visible shudder under their pure white habit. But I was the incurably greedy eclectic, needing to embrace the full A to Z spectrum of anything that appealed to me.

I sought to explain my eclecticism in respectable, scholarly terms, as if to tease the good nuns with an argument they would have difficulty in following. My affinity for the low end of the spectrum was not my fault,

I argued, since it was genetic, a biological inheritance from a long line of Hokkien ancestors who came to seek work in Singapore as low labourers. On the other hand, the affinity for the high end was an acquired trait, something I could be proud of, something learnt from my association with English-speaking natives who came to Singapore as culture bearers, not unschooled labourers. Thus the English language had admirably made up for its disreputable counterpart.

Between the two worlds, through a long process of internal argument, rationalisation and self-justification, with the English pun as starting point, I had become an insufferable, English-centric snob by the time I was a teenager.

Diligently pursuing the scientific knowledge that the English language had opened up for me, I convinced myself that there must be a specific gene for low humour, just as there was said to be a gene for intelligence, for musical talent, for the drinking habit, etc. It was probably embedded securely in the Y chromosome, since men had a greater propensity for coarse behaviour than women. I suspected that I had inherited this gene from my grandfather.

Ah Kong, who lived in Penang more than a hundred years ago, was an opium addict and was said to be in possession of the greatest repository of crude tales to share with whoever would listen to him as he puffed away at his opium pipe. He was also said to have the greatest arsenal of obscenities which he would hurl energetically at peddlers and beggars when they refused to go away. I heard an aunt recount an incident one afternoon when a scissors-and-knife-grinder came to the door, and insisted on a demonstration of his skills. When Ah Kong shouted at him to go away with some choice profanities, he responded with even choicer ones of his own, which impressed Ah Kong so much that he actually invited him in for a chat.

Ah Kong could pull bawdy tales out of thin air. A full moon? A squawking hen chased by a determined cockerel? The rice wine fermenting in the jar? The temple medium consulted by an anxious housewife? A large black mole at the corner of Fifth Aunt's right eye? The perennially pregnant household cat? Ah Kong could catch hold of any of these and spin a compelling tale around it, making us children giggle or press our hands to our mouths in suppressed laughter, while all the time listening wide-eyed, never missing a syllable. Ah Kong reminded me of the Ancient Mariner who held his audience captive as he told his stories with his hypnotically glittering eyes.

But unlike Ah Kong who went the whole way of dirt, I wanted to keep a clean distance from it. With a hypocrisy unusual for a youngster, I had a partiality for risqué tales, but at the same time was bent on giving the impression of the truly refined and pious, convent-bred young lady. It was a strategic hypocrisy that propelled me to join the circle of listeners around the unabashed, uninhibited story-telling Ah Kong but at the same time to put on an air of great indifference, looking on nonchalantly as the other children laughed uproariously. It was a double-faced stand that was probably brought about by the convent-instilled prudishness. I wanted to have my cake and eat it.

Later, I discovered, to my secret delight, that the versatile pun was able to serve that dual purpose easily. For it cleverly avoided the direct use of salacious words but brought them in by the back door by giving them a different dress. The *f* word? The various words for the various parts of male and female genitalia? Avoid them. Use instead those words that sound like them, or that merely hint at them, say these words slowly, archly, and the listener will immediately know what you are getting at, and burst into laughter.

Best of all, you haven't compromised your position. You're still part of civilised, polite society. You've ingeniously worked out a conspiracy of understanding with your listeners. Actually, this is possible whatever the language used, for every language has words that lend themselves easily to the wicked pun. This is because every language serves the entire range of human needs, including the very base and the very low. That means that every culture, through language, makes it possible to bring gutter humour into even the most polite society. Shakespeare was an expert at that.

Thus with delightful deviousness the pun could outwit social decorum, discomfiting Victorian prudes and delighting the rebels. It allowed vulgarity to come out in the open, disguised in refinement. In this way, one could have the best of both worlds. It allowed the prim convent product that was me to fuse with the libertine unable to shake off the convent influence; the disciplined public persona of Confucianist upbringing to cohabit with the private voyeur who had secretly read *Lady Chatterley's Lover*, then the most heavily censored novel; the lofty aesthete to reside comfortably with the incorrigible schlub. Ever the acquisitive *pau ka liow* seeker of knowledge and all pleasing things, I had found that the pun, perfectly reconciling these apparently contradictory attributes, was exactly the ally I wanted.

Freud explained the need for uninhibited laughter as the sudden release of libidinal energy, which presumably is a good thing. But then again, the father of psychology has been somewhat discredited, and his theories assigning a sexual origin to most pathologies have been dismissed as pure 'fraud-ianism', a cheap shot at a pun that doesn't really impress.

By now, I have a sizable collection of punny anecdotes of the raw, earthy kind which would have horrified my teachers, the convent nuns who had taught us to tell only edifying stories, and use only pure language. They might have compromised by approving the use of asterisks for 'sinful' words, a practice maintained by conservative mainstream newspapers that take pains over *sh***, *f**k*, ****hole*, etc. But they would definitely be scandalised by the open, liberal and joyous use of bold puns that I prefer to the apologetic asterisk, to celebrate life's earthy realities all the way.

When Donald Trump directly called Haiti and some poor African nations "shithole countries", he immediately provoked a storm of protest from the civilised world. Rude, crude, coarse, profane. Now if I were Trump, I would have cleverly clothed my natural scatological tendencies with a clever pun. I would have avoided the direct vulgar reference to the countries I despised, and instead co-opted the cunningly elliptical pun. For instance, I would have said, in calm tones and with a straight face, that I didn't want immigrants from 'the Turd World', that I didn't care for 'Close Encounters of the Turd Kind'.

I suspect the pun would have been equally effective in speech or print. It would have provoked a mix of surprise, mild shock, some puzzlement, perhaps even some secret delight. There would also have been delayed responses, as not everyone would be familiar with the term and would have to go running to their dictionaries which, if they maintained the unfailing British austerity of the Oxford Dictionary, would have warned against the vulgar slanginess of the term. Such a medley of responses would certainly have muted the storm of outrage, perhaps even dispelled it.

There might even be enough provocative innuendo in the pun to challenge journalists to come up with their own ingenious use of this special figure of speech, where the language is at one level cleaned of all crudity but at another, is saturated with it, in ways that only the fecund expressiveness of the English pun allows. It really does allow you to have your cake and eat it. To be and not to be. To be wickedly frivolous and not to be seen as such.

Trump had, alas, through his singularly direct, unmediated and uninspired expression of his lavatorial instincts, missed out on the opportunity to engage with the marvellous comedic resources of the English language.

The Daffodil Syndrome

I used to hang around the edges of adult conversation, convinced that the sporadic bursts of laughter from my mother, the neighbours or the maidservants were caused by some particularly salacious gossip. I couldn't of course understand all that they were talking about, but knew enough to want to hear more, for instance, about an elderly neighbour whose nickname meant 'Old Lecher' and his young, giggly mistress, fifty years his junior, whose nickname was 'Gatal', a Malay word meaning 'itch'. I wanted to hear, too, about the neighbourhood's greatest, fastest purveyor of gossip, a seamstress whose nickname of 'Tali-gelem' was a Hokkien corruption of 'telegram'.

"Shoo, go away," my mother would say. "Young people mustn't listen in on adult talk." Which of course made me even more curious.

I thought that in the regular composition writing lessons in school, I could write a story about Old Lecher or Tali-gelem. But I never did. Instead I wrote a story about an English farmer named Mr Whittington who lived on a large farm with many sheep and a lovely apple orchard.

My mother and her friends were, one afternoon, light-heartedly talking about a certain neighbour whom we children addressed as Ah Guek Soh. Poor Ah Guek Soh's predicament was known throughout the neighbourhood and beyond. Keen to have a son right from the start of her marriage, she had had five daughters in a row, each disappointment only serving to strengthen her determination to try once again.

Then she went into hospital for her sixth child, and hey presto! It was a boy at last. Almost immediately the rumours started spreading, but only in whispers, behind cupped hands: It was another female, not a male. The newborn girl had been quickly taken away and replaced by a newborn boy, apparently at great expense. A few days later, Ah Guek Soh and her baby left the hospital. She gave him the affectionate nickname of 'Boy Boy' and celebrated his first month with a lavishness never seen for any of her five girls. She talked endlessly about how her prayers to *Ti Kong* or Sky God had been granted, and everybody congratulated her effusively but, behind her back, whispered unkindly about the baby-swopping on the hospital bed. The whispers had it that Ah Guek Soh had to pawn all the jewellery that her mother had given her on her marriage, in order to pay for the baby boy.

For composition writing one day, we were required to write a story about an interesting neighbour. I wanted to do a composition on Ah Guek Soh, but instead wrote on a Mrs Chester-Brown who lived in a cottage in the woods that were always full of buttercups in spring.

It would be years before I was cured of the Daffodil Syndrome. With the English language had come English culture which, in those days, comprised all I read about in story books chosen by an Irish nun, Sister St Alban, for our small class library. I became enamoured of castles and elves and princesses with long golden tresses and princes who came riding on white horses.

Later, with the same delight, I plunged into the world created by possibly the most successful children's writer of that period, Enid Blyton, moving from her stories about the little lovable Noddy to those of an adventuresome group of young teenagers called 'The Famous Five'. I saved whatever little pocket money I had to buy the Enid Blyton books (in those days they were all hardcover and pretty expensive) and spent hours joining the adventurers track smugglers, trap robbers, find gold hidden deep in caves, discover mysterious caves hidden deep inside cliffs.

I loved the poem 'The Brook' by Lord Alfred Tennyson, learning it by heart, revelling in lines such as *I come from haunts of coot and hern* with no idea whatsoever of what coot and hern could be. I enjoyed the lilting light-heartedness of the refrain: *For men may come and men may go/ But I go on forever*. It was a line that could be repeated endlessly, for the sheer pleasure of its rhythm.

But the poem I loved best was Wordsworth's 'The Daffodils'. Sister St Alban pinned up on the classroom noticeboard a picture of a field of daffodils, exactly as Wordsworth had described them, dancing and swaying in the breeze. I thought that they were the most beautiful flowers I had ever seen. *Ten thousand saw I at a glance/ Tossing their heads in sprightly dance*. I couldn't imagine the local hibiscus or frangipani doing that.

I once wrote a composition for which Sister gave me a full ten marks upon ten. I was elated! Never before had I earned a perfect score in any classroom written exercise. When my exercise book was returned, I read my composition again and again, together with Sister's comment of 'Very Good' written in her neat hand. For the first time, Sister was unambiguously complimentary. Her usual comments of 'Nearly Very Good', or 'Very Nearly Good', attesting to a mind overly fond of fine distinctions, often had mine mightily puzzled as I tried to figure out which was a better grade. But this time there was no need for any puzzling out. My composition was a straight winner!

What had put Sister in such a generous grade-giving mood? She had given us the title 'The Happiest Day' for that day's composition writing exercise. I instantly and effortlessly wrote about a day of picnicking in the woods in spring, picking and eating strawberries, beside a babbling brook. I described in detail the azure spring sky, the gentle spring breeze caressing my face and wafting my hair, the gurgling sound of the brook soothing my ears, the sweet taste of strawberry in my mouth. I had never seen a strawberry in my life, much less tasted one, but I wrote about that gustatory pleasure so convincingly that it must have brought some nostalgia to Sister, as must have the references to the seasonal and countryside pleasures of her girlhood in Ireland.

Later, as a writer, I would ask myself, with no small degree of embarrassment: Why hadn't I written about something closer to home — the hawker centres, the market, the people of my little hometown of Kulim? After all, they were all around me in my growing-up years, inseparable from my everyday life, embedded in my very consciousness. I certainly could have written confidently about this real world of mine, using the English language that I was already competent in.

Alas, I think I was ashamed to do so. I was suffering from some inferiority complex, and believed that to use the great English language to write about the old *humsub* neighbour or Tali-gelem or that silly superstition warning against praising a baby openly in the hearing of jealous, evil spirits, would be a desecration of that glorious language, or at the least, a show of discourtesy. My mother often quoted a Hokkien proverb against the inappropriate use of a sophisticated instrument for a trivial purpose: 'Never use a knife meant for killing a buffalo to decapitate a chicken.' Such a waste. I would have to use a far more powerful idiom to convey the sheer incongruity of using the illustrious English language for my inferior local subjects.

Fortunately, in my adult years, I could free myself, once and for all, from this dreadful influence of the Daffodil Syndrome, and fling open the gates of creativity to set free a huge repository of local tales that had been needlessly held back. Now they rush out, in a torrent, ready to be told.

A Murder of Crows?
A Kettle of Hawks?

I'm amused by the English eccentrics that I read about, including an aristocratic lady who dressed like an Arab woman and lived in the desert, and an aristocratic gentleman who was so reclusive that he had his food passed to him through a slot in the door, so that he didn't have to face his servants.

But I'm awed, not amused, by the eccentricity of the English language. I'm utterly fascinated by the countless peculiarities, irregularities and illogicalities of the rules governing its usage. Indeed, these rules can be so complex, involving so many exceptions, that they are better learnt in the breach than in the observance.

As children, we must have faithfully learnt, for instance, the rule governing the formation of plural forms by simply adding s, such as in 'boys', 'dogs', 'pictures', etc, only to be flummoxed by the exceptions of 'mice', 'geese', 'oxen', 'women', 'children,' 'formulae', 'indices'. Then there were animal nouns that had no plural form: sheep, deer, moose, fish, salmon, antelope, elk. Mercifully, these formed a short list that could be easily memorised.

Later as a writer, I would cheerfully apply this s plural formation rule to the Hokkien words I sometimes used in my stories. Hokkien has no provision for plural forms, but I thought that certain colourful ones which I used freely in my wickedly satirical stories about dirty old men could be thus anglicised and made more exotic: 'Uncle Or Kee (or Uncle Black Mole), easily one of the best known *humsubs* in the neighbourhood, would often stare at pretty, well-endowed young women drawing water from the well, all the while languorously stroking the five long hairs that drooped from the large mole on his chin. Actually there were two other equally lascivious, outsized *kees*, one on each earlobe.'

If you came from a native language that has no markers, not only for the plural form, but for the tenses to indicate the past, present or future of an action, then it would really be uphill work learning English with its many inflections. Hokkien is happily unburdened by any need to inflect the verb to indicate that the action took place in the past — you just needed to add the suffix *liow* meaning 'already'. *Wa chia, Wa chia liow* for 'I eat', 'I have eaten'.

Very enthusiastic about the English language, I overdid the learning, and mentally applied its past tense rule to Hokkien verbs, as I had applied the plural form rule to Hokkien nouns. The result was strange linguistic concoctions such as *Wa chia-ed liow*. If I was using colloquial Malay, a lingua franca alongside Hokkien, the freak sentence would be 'I have *makan-ed* already.' It was as if through the process of anglicising Hokkien and Malay grammar, I was giving it a patina of English formality and dignity.

But if you are a besotted anglophile like myself, one who had actually suffered from the Daffodil Syndrome for years, all the intricacies of the language are of no consequence. I love the English language so much that no degree of eccentricity can put me off. Indeed, I see the unpredictability and whimsicality of the language as a mark of its uniqueness, its fancifulness and peculiarities as offerings on love's altar. If there are difficulties, they are just hurdles to be readily overcome on the way to the love feast.

It had not always been that way.

I had an English language teacher who, for some reason, was obsessed by lists and believed she could teach best by presenting long lists to her students to memorise, whether these were of grammatical rules, proverbs, synonyms and antonyms, prefixes and suffixes. The longer the list, the better. I suspect Teacher had sadistically discovered a method of teaching English that was wondrously easy for her and infernally difficult for the forty students she had to face every day.

In particular, she was obsessed by collective nouns. She came up with a very long list which she patiently wrote out on the blackboard and also on a large sheet of paper pinned up on the classroom noticeboard. She gave us a specific time to learn the full list of nouns by heart, after which we would have to, one by one, go to the front of the class to recite it to the whole class. Entire teaching periods were devoted to our silently memorising these nouns, while Teacher sat at her table, idly gazing around, fiddling with her hair, her fingernails. She was a very contented teacher. She promised us that the one who got all the collective nouns right would get a prize.

From the start, I had strong reservations about the list we had been given. It was a very long and very strange list. Many of the collective nouns made no sense to me, but I didn't dare ask Teacher what they meant. I had no problem with a team of oxen, or a shoal of herring or even a colony of penguins, but puzzled mightily over an army of caterpillars, a tribe of antelopes, a busyness of ferrets, a parliament of rooks, a shrewdness of apes.

I tried to understand the rationale behind each odd noun. Maybe it was a natural human tendency to anthropomorphise, to project human attributes on to animals (and even inanimate objects) to understand them better. An army of caterpillars? Maybe these little humble creatures had the ability to organise themselves, like us, for battle. A parliament of rooks? Maybe even birds could come together to discuss and negotiate, like democratic citizens.

But a murder of crows? Crows were black birds associated with misfortune, but who did the murdering here? The crows or a human agent? In any case, 'murder' as a collective noun provided no clue as to what the actual grouping looked like.

A kettle of hawks? It conjured up a very odd picture. Dead hawks crammed into a super big kettle? Why this common domestic utensil which surely had nothing to do with birds of prey?

I had to learn even weirder collective nouns: an ambush of tigers, a committee of raccoons, a crash of rhinoceroses, a shiver of sharks. It was impossible to get behind the rationale for the origin of these collective nouns. Then, even more bizarrely, there were some collective nouns with names that I could not find in any dictionary: a smuth of jellyfish, a dule of doves, a sedge of cranes. For goodness' sake, where had Teacher got all these words from?

It was as if some committee in Great Britain, appointed by some language authority and tasked to come up with terms for animals that humans liked to see gathered in orderly groups, had got riotously drunk and then begun competing with each other to come up with anything that came into their heads. The crazier, the better. When their list was complete, the language authority published it in a Teachers' Handbook that became an instant hit.

Suddenly the sheer nonsensicality of it overwhelmed me. I became impatient and wanted answers. Rather boldly, I approached Teacher with two questions: Why were the collective nouns not in the dictionary? What was the use of learning words that we would never ever use? I surprised myself by my boldness. I told her I probably would never see a penguin in my life, much less a colony of them.

Teacher looked rather surprised, frowned a little, then told me stiffly that if I wished, I could learn just half the list of collective nouns, not the full one. By now much emboldened I asked: Could I choose that half? She said 'yes' impatiently and then signalled to me to return to my seat. I knew what I wanted to do, to solve, once and for all, the vexatious problem of this whole silly exercise of memorising a long list of collective nouns that must have originated in some collectively lunatic heads.

The nouns I carefully chose for my halved list comprised only those animals, about twenty in all, whose groupings were easily taken care of by just a handful of sensible, easy-to-learn collective nouns: herd, flock, pack, swarm, shoal, troop. These group nouns could cover any animal — one as large as an elephant or as small as a mosquito, any creature that crawled or swam or flew. Surely the English language should have observed the basic law of economy and stopped at these instead of going on a wild rampage of semantic nonsense?

That was the first time that my romance with the language had floundered a little.

I would later find out that this chaos of collective nouns, all related to animals, probably originated in the medieval ages and could be blamed on an aristocracy fond of hunting. Or they could have originated with medieval monks fond of meditating on the beauty of creation and suddenly galvanised by some spiritual impulse to focus on the divinity of even low or obscure forms of animal life, as seen in the following collective nouns which have a distinctly religious connotation: a congregation of alligators, a candle of anteaters, a blessing of narwal. Why would anyone want to know the name of a rare species of whale found in the Arctic, much less the group name when it came together in large numbers, if it ever did? I suspect that the good monks wanted to emphasise the inclusive, divinely-inspired magnanimity of Noah when he gathered together all those animals to lead into his ark before God unleashed the Great Flood over the Earth. Noah demonstrated this thoughtful inclusiveness by not leaving out the little-known narwal.

Beyond the initial irritation, I found collective nouns to be a harmless eccentricity of the English language. But there were some that made me sit up and take notice.

They were those that were far from arbitrary; they actually showed creative wit and true inventiveness, and they were probably of recent origin.

From these, I have selected a few favourites. They have nothing to do with animals, and everything to do with the endlessly interesting human species. Actually they refer to a profession that has no use for collective nouns, since the modus operandi more suitably involves only the single individual, for maximum assurance of privacy and discretion. For prostitutes seldom operate in groups except perhaps when they want to demonstrate against government policies unfair to them, such as a new income tax regulation targeted at their earnings.

My favourite collective nouns for prostitutes do not at all reflect the reality of their lives, but are based purely on the use of my favourite figure of speech, the pun. I wish that the wondrously creative pun could have come up with more than just three examples: an anthology of pros, a blare of strumpets, a whorde of hookers. When I first came upon them, I thought, wow, I wish I could have come up with such stunning punning.

As for the list-loving teacher, she was not finished yet. She imposed on us another long list, this time of English idioms that she said were necessary to improve our use of the English language. The idioms seemed both culturally alien and alienating to me. There was a plethora of idioms referring to food items that were almost never seen on our dining tables: 'to eat humble pie', 'to butter up', 'to bring home the bacon', 'a red herring'. (I'd never eaten herring in my life, much less red herring.) The food idioms for people were also just as culturally irrelevant to Asians:

'a rotten apple', 'a tough cookie', 'an egghead', 'a couch potato'. I could apply 'tough cookie' to several of my strong-minded female friends, but couldn't visualise them breaking up easily, like cookies crumbling between the fingers, melting in the mouth.

Indeed, I depended a great deal on my visualising ability in the learning process, and found much difficulty in picturing an idle, happy-go-lucky uncle who never gave his wife enough money for her housekeeping, 'bringing home the bacon'. Aunt would have been nonplussed by Uncle bringing home a food item that was completely unfamiliar to her. She would have sniffed it suspiciously and then thrown it away in disgust. So mentally I changed 'bacon' to the items she would have appreciated Uncle spending his salary on, to bring home to his large, needy family: rice, flour, cooking oil, soya sauce, sugar, firewood, kerosene. The closest Asian equivalent to 'bringing home the bacon' would be 'filling the rice bowl'.

Years ago, there was a colleague, a teacher of English and literature, who was suddenly, unaccountably seized with a nationalistic fervour that made him denounce the learning of English idioms and proverbs which made no sense to local children. He said it was pure imperialistic nonsense. "Why do we still have this colonial hangover?" he demanded, looking round at us in the school staffroom, as we sat marking exercise books, sipping coffee, relaxing.

He advocated replacing these idioms with locally relevant ones. "Why not replace 'bread and butter' with 'rice and curry', 'a rotten apple' with a familiar local fruit, like a banana or mango or a chiku? 'Keeping up with the Joneses'? Hah! Why not 'keeping up with the Tans or Lees'?"

He argued that since the dog was an animal that was a taboo in Malay culture, the popular English idioms featuring dogs should be banned. "Get rid of 'dog in a manger', 'let sleeping dogs lie'." He said with sudden inspiration: "Why not replace 'dog' with 'cat'? After all, the cat is a popular Malay choice for a household pet. A cat in a manger. Let sleeping cats lie. Man's best friend."

But he reckoned without those idioms about dogs which were not at all canine-friendly: 'dog-eat-dog world', 'dog days', 'gone to the dogs'. Their replacement by the much loved cat would have elicited strong disapproval from the Malay community.

The colleague's campaign was, as could be expected, short-lived. In any case, none of us ever bothered to listen long enough to ask questions or offer comments. Soon he gave up, with a final mocking grunt as he read from a students' manual called *Enrich Your English*: "To take coals to Newcastle. A penny for your thoughts. Mighty oaks from little acorns grow. Hah! No wonder we never progress as a nation!"

The moral lesson of this real-life anecdote: Never attempt to tamper with English idioms and proverbs, whatever their eccentricity and cultural irrelevance, because they are here to stay. Indeed, never attempt to tamper with any aspect of the English language. For it is an organism that has grown steadily and spontaneously over a long period of time, taking on a shape, character and essence that is entirely its own, so that any attempt to change it in any way invariably fails. For the truth is that language is not a top-down creation that can be altered, but a bottom-up development that has an internal dynamic and life of its own. The English language in particular was born, and grew, in the most fertile of soils. If it is an eccentric language, that eccentricity is part of its rich and complex history.

And never ever try to rationalise eccentricity, because it is a mark of creativity. Indeed the two are inextricably linked, fused into a single entity that exists in its own right, with special claims of its own that are beyond the reach of reason. That is its ultimate strength. The renowned English thinker of the Enlightenment, John Stuart Mill, goes so far as to assert that eccentricity is vital for a society to reach the highest levels of intellectual and moral excellence: "The amount of eccentricity in a society has generally been proportional to the amount of genius, mental vigour and moral courage which it contained."

Singapore would be a little ambivalent in its response to Mill. Used to ranking rationality over emotion, communality over individuality, consensus over private opinion, it is nevertheless beginning to encourage creativity, in its awareness that it has to keep up with a rapidly changing world. But the version of creativity it is comfortable with, has still to show some of the old discipline. It cannot be the freewheeling type, bearing the marks of idiosyncrasy or worse, eccentricity. To Mill's clarion call to all nations to be eccentric if they truly want to be great, Singapore might say, with characteristic caution, "Our society is not yet ready." Even the most liberal-minded Singaporean would have offered, at best, only two cheers for eccentricity.

A Girl Named Bamboo

Ah Leng Kia as usual led the others in taunting us as we made our way to school, our satchels strapped to our backs. There were four of them that day, in their usual dirty singlets and ragged black cotton pants, in various poses of relaxation on an abandoned bullock cart. We looked down as we walked on steadily to the convent school that we attended, ignoring the whistles, catcalls, the exaggerated hissing sounds of *ffft ffft* and *sssh sssh* that were supposed to mark English speech.

Ah Leng Kia went beyond the sounds to discharge a medley of English words and phrases that he had picked up, which, if shouted out in a certain way, could be taken for expletives. *Your mar-der and your far-der, yah! Your gand-farder head. I no go, you no come. I say, you say.* Sometimes they sang out, with much derisive laughter, the British national anthem that we were required to sing every morning at school during assembly, just before lessons began. *God shave our kay-shus king, long leev our no-ba king, God shave the king.* His companions joined him, making obscene gestures with their fingers.

My siblings and I whispered to each other, "Jealous, that's what they are. Jealous like hell." We continued, in high-pitched mocking imitation of the ignoramus' struggling pronunciation. "They vell-ee jealous, I tell you, and we vell-ee soll-ee for them!" The ingrained inability of the Chinese-educated to pronounce the *r* sound which rolled so easily on our tongues, was a source of real gratification. Products of Chinese-medium schools, they would end up as the inferior majority depending, for their livelihood as coffeeshop attendants, hawkers and office cleaners, on the superior minority they were now mocking.

We called them the 'I say, you say' crowd, not only because it was the only grammatically correct English phrase they could manage, but also because of the Hokkien meaning of the verb. It means 'wash', allowing the 'I say, you say' phrase to be expanded into a two-line verse using a crude Hokkien term to refer to 'backside': *I say, you say/ Kar chooi bo say*, translated roughly into *I wash, you wash/ Backside not washed*, the disgusting habit presumably attributed to the unwelcome foreigners and their English-educated sycophants.

Ah Leng Kia liked one of our maidservants enough to sometimes stop by the kitchen door and chat with her, whispering the *I say, you say* joke to her to make her laugh. But Ah Teik, whose name meant Bamboo, never joined in the laughter. All her energies were concentrated on the goal of moving away, once and for all, from precisely that low world represented by Ah Leng Kia and her fellow maidservants. The world she wanted to get herself into was that of the English-educated, with their refined minds and manners. And the single most important signifier of that refinement was the language they spoke. Ah Teik became a committed self-taught learner of the English language.

She was one of the 'bondmaids' or *char bor kan* who had been given to my grandmother by their impoverished mothers when they were small children. Through the years, a stream of distraught women had appeared on Grandmother's doorstep with their tiny, undernourished daughters, offering them, not for adoption, but permanent possession. When Grandmother accepted their offers, they expressed their gratitude, and when she offered a small *ang pow*, they shook their heads vigorously. "No, no," they would say with effusive humility. "How can I take your money? Your kindness is enough."

Grandmother, who lived in Penang, had clear plans for the girls as soon as they came into her house. As they grew up, they were either put to do the housework in her large household or, if they were skilled with their fingers, to help out in her thriving home business, which was the making of beautifully embroidered, beaded slippers traditionally worn by brides. The maids assigned this work spent hours over piles of small beads, separating them according to size, shape and colour, and then sewing them on to silk or satin, under Grandmother's strict supervision.

Grandmother had so many of these maids that she could afford to pass some of them on to her three children to serve as their servants, invariably giving them stern advice about working hard and not causing any trouble in their new homes.

Ah Teik came to us under these circumstances. From the start she resented her lowly position, but managed to combine the deferential demeanour expected of a maid with an underlying defiance that was all her own. The tension resulted in a permanent frown on the forehead that was at odds with the extended smile on her lips.

Her entire demeanour made it clear to everyone, without her uttering a single word, that she was made for better things, by virtue of her superior mind and her affinity for the English language and all the good things it brought into her world. These comprised the English songs that were played daily on Rediffusion, the English movies that were shown regularly in the town's only cinema, the English comic books that could be bought at the town's main bookshop, even the daily English newspaper that my father subscribed to. They were Ah Teik's mainstay.

"Who does she think she is?" my older sisters would say with exasperation. They could tolerate *char bor kan* who flirted with the coffeeshop attendant next door, or were occcasionally slack in their work or who, if they were entrusted to do the daily shopping at the market, helped themselves to a few cents from the shopping money to buy their favourite *kuey* there, making sure to gulp down the delicious stuff and wipe their mouths before reaching home. But my sisters had no patience with *char bor kan* who put on airs and had pretensions to the world of the English-educated that they could never belong to.

Ah Teik picked up English very quickly by carefully listening to the conversations going on around her, even if they were coded. "Be careful. Bamboo is watching us," one of my sisters would say, lowering her voice and giving her a sideways glance. "Let's go to the other room." Or "Why is she picking up the newspaper?" "Did you hear that — she's listening to Rediffusion again and singing *Sipping Soda*!"

Ah Teik sang softly, but loud enough to be heard, with just the right degree of arrogant defiance: *See-ping sota, see-eeping sota/ We see-ping sota tloo a stlaw!* Rediffusion was her most trusted teacher of correct English pronunciation and very soon, through dogged perseverance, her speech was cleared of all the awkward features of the struggling learner. Her pronunciation, in particular, improved so rapidly that, to my sisters' great annoyance, she was even practising her English on visitors. "Good afternoon, Miss Rajeswary. You want cup of coffee? Good morning, Mr Boon Chai. How are you today? Goodbye, Mr Boon Chai, please come again."

Boon Chai, who was a frequent visitor and hopeful suitor of my eldest sister, remarked to her, "Hey, your maid is speaking better English than me." My sister was furious. She forbade Ah Teik to speak to all her visitors in future. Ah Teik responded with an arch smile. She was confident that her various skills of deducing meaning from speakers' intonation, repetition of certain words, contextual clues, facial expressions and gestures, would soon enable her to speak English with a competence that could match that of anyone in the household. "Just you all wait and see," she would say to herself, again with that enigmatic smile.

"How dare she wear that dress?"

Ah Teik had bought a short red dress with a frilly collar and puffed sleeves which she wore with serene self-consciousness as she went about the housework, disregarding the unwritten rule that *char bor kan* were to dress appropriately, in modestly sleeved blouses and loose trousers or sarong.

"Where did she get those 'Film Fun' comics from?" "Did you notice her pretending to smile at the Laurel and Hardy comics, as if she understood the jokes?" "She went to see that Errol Flynn film without permission? How dare she!" Errol Flynn had become Ah Teik's model of the ideal male, handsome and debonair, beside whom the likes of Ah Leng Kia were just so much rubbish to be disposed of.

The exasperation mounted in a rapid escalation of complaints. My mother decided to send Ah Teik back to Grandmother after she saw her doing a deliberately slow sweeping of the spaces around my father's chair in his office in the front portion of the house, a pert smile on her face, dressed in the notorious short frilly dress.

Ah Teik had asked me, months before she left, to teach her to write her name. She carefully copied out the letters I had duly written on a sheet of paper torn from my school exercise book, gripping the pencil tightly, her brow furrowed in concentration. She wanted me to teach her how to write both names, 'Ah Teik' as well as 'Bamboo'. "I know they call me Bamboo," she said. "They think I don't know, but I can understand everything!"

She practised writing both names on the blank spaces of old newspapers, and on the blank sides of the small squares of paper from the Chinese a-page-a-day wall calendar that were torn off daily, to mark the progression of the year. The paper was no bigger than a child's palm, but Ah Teik made good use of it. The last time I saw her was when she was practising writing her name in flowing script, rather than the childish block letters, on one of those calendar pages. She showed it to me proudly.

Her story was a most tragic one. After she was sent back to Grandmother, her own mother who had not seen her for years, came and took her home. Ah Teik had a twin brother who, in the unspeakable squalor of their living conditions, shared a mattress on the floor with her at night, in a room crowded with other sleepers. She became pregnant with his child. They continued to live with the mother as a de facto couple, going on to have several more children. Nobody knew what eventually happened to them.

I remember Ah Teik most vividly not for her awful fate but, strangely, for her dogged attempts to learn the English language. She saw it as her salvation, and it eluded her. It could have saved her. Years later, as a writer, I wrote a story about a poor village girl who was rewarded for her unflinching efforts to improve her lot through an English education. I called my protagonist 'Bamboo Girl' because this distinctive tropical plant symbolised, aptly, the resilience and toughness that never failed her when it had, alas, failed poor Ah Teik.

She moved softly to take her usual place outside the classroom, pressed against the wall, close to the open window, but with her body bent almost double to make sure the top of her head would not be visible to the teacher or anyone in the classroom. She knew the English language lesson was about to begin, and she waited to hear the teacher's voice come floating out of the window, straight to her alert ears. The teacher was Sister St Philomena who was so good in her teaching that anyone could learn easily by just paying attention to her. She didn't understand the meaning of many words that Sister used, but by memorising them and repeating them to herself at home, she could understand them the next time Sister used them.

She was quivering with excitement now because she loved the story that Sister St Philomena was telling. She was sure it had a special meaning, something to do with family love. It was a pity that she had to leave before the story ended, as she had to go to the marketplace to help out at her father's bee hoon stall. But she could guess the ending, and could later check if it was the correct one, should Sister refer to the story again.

"What are you doing here?" The school gardener approached her frowning, a cigarette between his surly lips, and made signs of dismissal. She was about to say something but he waved her off impatiently. His hostile eyes followed her as she walked slowly towards the school gate. Panic gripped her. She could no longer have her English language lessons outside Sister's classroom! Oh no, that would be the end of her dreams. But wait, she had a bright idea.

In the next few nights — she could not spare the day hours that had to be spent doing housework or helping her father at his stall — she went to town and began to search around the areas surrounding the hawkers' stalls, the stores, the bicycle parks, the town's bar, any place where men could be expected to visit and, if they smoked, to drop their cigarette butts. Her eyes were quick to spot the butts. In three days she had picked up more than fifty which she put in a small paper bag.

At home, alone by herself, in the light of a small kerosene lamp, she carefully tore open each butt and extracted every bit of tobacco from it. The total amount was quite sizable.

She put it in an empty cigarette tin which she presented to the school gardener the next day. He looked at it, saw that the amount would serve for at least ten home-made cigarettes, and took the tin from her, without saying a word.

The next morning she was back at her place outside Sister's classroom. The gardener pretended not to see her, as he sat under a tree, smoking.

Sister's clear voice floated out of the window. She was asking a question related to a previous lesson. None of her pupils in the classroom could answer it. "I'm going to give you just two minutes to give me the right answer," said Sister severely. Suddenly she saw a girl, wearing the ragged clothes and rubber slippers of the typical kampong dweller, bursting into the classroom, and saying excitedly, "I know! I know!"

And Bamboo Girl did indeed know the answer, which she rattled off expertly and breathlessly in front of the astonished Sister St Philomena and her class of forty pupils. Looking incredulous, Sister asked her another question, and another, and another, based on previous lessons, and she could answer them all. Sister stared at her. She demanded to know what it was all about, and Bamboo Girl told her story.

Looking very excited, Sister told her to wait, and almost ran to the office of the principal of the school, Sister St John. Together they quizzed Bamboo Girl, peppering her with questions about her parents, her siblings, her home life, what gave her the idea to learn by stationing herself outside Sister St Philomena's classroom, how long she had been doing this.

Sister St John said with grim purpose, "She must be allowed to have a proper education, I'll see to it." The next day, accompanied by a teacher who could translate English into Hokkien, she visited Bamboo Girl's father. He had never seen a western nun before, much less a stern-looking one who looked as if she was not afraid of anybody. All he could do was smile nervously, make some unintelligible sounds, and nod each time the formidable female looked him straight in the eyes.

"So it is settled," said Sister St John firmly. "Tell the father his daughter will be enrolled straightaway in my school, and placed in Sister St Philomena's class. Sister will give her whatever coaching she needs, to fit in. Tell the father also," in a softening tone, "that his daughter will be a pride to him and to all her teachers."

Singlish? "Certainly Not!" "Aiyah, Okay, Lah!"

Singapore must be the only one among former British colonies where the English language has had an uninterrupted history of support from the government, where it has been the official and dominant language of the schools, educational institutions, the courts, government administration and the media. Where the language had elsewhere suffered setbacks, decline or even expulsion, English has not only been fully adopted but nurtured to the stage where it is an ineradicable part of Singapore life and culture.

The reason for this unique position of English in Singapore has nothing to do with sentiment and everything to do with pragmatics. Indeed, it is the special brand of pragmatism that was the distinctive characteristic of the first prime minister, Mr Lee Kuan Yew.

While newly independent countries such as India or Malaysia were saying to the English language, "We have taken down the British flag. Now we want to take you down too", Mr Lee was saying, "No, we want you to stay. Not because we love you, but because we need you. We need you for trade and business in the international community, we need you to tap into the world of science and technology, we need you to function in the world of diplomacy and most of all, we need you as the means of inter-ethnic communication in our very diverse society. There is no other language that would be acceptable to the three major races of the Chinese, the Indians and the Malays."

And so it has been the rise and rise of English in Singapore.

But its offspring Singlish (short for 'Singapore English') has not had such unambiguous support. Like its counterparts, including Indian English, Malaysian English, Jamaican English and Filipino English, it is often seen as an inferior version of its parent, having become too localised to be of any use to anyone except its local users. The different Englishes that have arisen, that reflect the speech patterns of the indigenous tongues, are said to be completely unintelligible to one another, as they have long been to the native English speaker. Tourists from the UK and the US say they have difficulty understanding Singapore's salesgirls, shop assistants, airline stewardesses, the man in the street.

It is precisely because of this crucial role of English in international trade, business and the tourism industry that there have been 'Speak Good English' campaigns in Singapore, spanning decades now, that are subtly aimed at the rooting out of Singlish or, at least, at reducing its unintelligibility to foreign visitors. At one time, the campaigns were taken very seriously because the problem was seen as no less than a major national issue, with the result that mainstream institutions such as the schools and the media felt obliged to play their roles.

Thus teachers became language watchdogs, making sure that even in the playground their students did not speak Singlish. (One overly conscientious school, it was said, imposed a fine for each mistake overheard by teachers who doubled up as language vigilantes during the recess when students tended to be careless in their speech.) The media ran special 'Correct English' columns that identified common mistakes made by Singaporeans. Heads of departments in government organisations were tasked to oversee and edit memos and reports, especially those that went up to ministerial level and would come under the sharp eyes of arguably Singapore's best English speaker, Mr Lee Kuan Yew.

The drive for correctness pleased the purists (people like the ungenerously satirised Dr John Thong in a previous story) who believed that the Queen's English should be the ultimate goal, that Singlish was an ugly blot on the fair face of English, and should thus be eradicated. No, said the linguists, eradication is not possible because Singlish is a natural, spontaneous development in the long history of English use in Singapore and is now a fixed feature in the country's linguistic landscape. To try to uproot it would be as unrealistic as trying to alter the physical landscape.

Suddenly, with the assertion that Singlish was here to stay, came a flood of claims for its merits. It was said to have much *social* value, linking the highly-educated upper classes with the not-so-educated lower classes: When the professionals spoke Singlish to their maids or gardeners, sales assistants, grocers, shopkeepers, etc, there was this social glue at work. It was also said to have *political* value:

Singlish, being a unifying language among the different ethnic groups, could be the very means for forging a political identity that would be necessary for a small country wedged between two larger, not always friendly, neighbours. Lastly, and not least, Singlish could have great *literary* value: It could be the expressive tool of writers wishing to produce a distinctive Singapore literature, to write, at last, the Great Singapore Novel.

There arose then two opposing camps, the first vilifying Singlish and actually calling it a bastardised variety of English, and the second canonising it as the offspring that surpassed its parent.

I confess that for a while I was much troubled by the confusion surrounding Singlish. My varied experiences with regard to the English language had contributed to my own confusion. I had been a teacher of the language in secondary schools, determined to root out all the mistakes of Singlish that my students were making, in order to get them to pass that all-important English language exam in the Cambridge-GCE O-Level examination. I was also a teacher of English literature, struggling to make my students appreciate the sophisticated complexity of Shakespearean English when they were still grappling with the basics of English grammar.

I had, moreover, approached the study of English as an academic, having done a postgraduate study on the attitudes of Singaporeans towards standard English and Singlish, with the strict objectivity required of the researcher. Finally, I had become one of the first local writers in Singapore using English to describe local events and people, and had discovered, to my delight, that, whatever the negative attitudes towards it, Singlish could be wonderfully exploited for literary purposes.

Here was a mixed bag indeed! One part of me decried Singlish; another liked it immensely. Singlish had made me quite schizoid.

Then I saw where my problem lay. It was in treating 'bad English' and 'Singlish' as one and the same thing. They are not, and should never be conflated. Bad English is the result of incomplete learning of the language, when the rules of usage have not been properly taught or learnt. As a consequence, a variety loosely called 'pidgin' develops, characterised by oversimplified English grammar and other elements such as pronunciation taken from local languages, notably colloquial Hokkien and Malay.

Singlish, in the sense that I'm using here, has nothing to do with incomplete and faulty learning behind bad English. If it bears some of the marks of bad English, for instance, in its incorrect pronunciation and grammar, these are actually a deliberate device used by competent speakers to achieve a certain *social* purpose. For instance, speakers switch from using standard English to colloquial Singlish, from a formal to an informal tone, to establish a friendly atmosphere, in order to put people at their ease, to inject a note of cordiality, to initiate humour. When the competent speaker code-switches in this way, the Singlish he uses is perfectly intelligible to his interlocutors. His code-switching ability, enabling him to make full use of the entire range of speech registers along the social speech spectrum, effortlessly gliding up and down as the situation requires, makes him a consummate speaker of the language.

When my friends and I play mahjong, we inject Singlish liberally into our normal standard English, creating an atmosphere of camaraderie and goodwill, as befits a non-competitive game: "*I can't believe my run of bad luck! Hey, Mag, why you so stingy? Can't let me pong even once, eh?*" "*Stop complaining. My luck's just as bad. Aiyoh, haven't game once this round. For next round, we shuffle the tiles properly, okay?*"

Our Dr John Thong seems capable only of the formal register, speaking in impeccable Queen's English on all occasions, hence reflecting a real language incompetence. Suppose he has a brother, Dr Robert Thong, who is the opposite, showing the ability to use the entire range of speech registers, in response to differing social contexts. Imagine a day in Dr Robert Thong's life where he has to continually code-switch:

In the morning, Dr Robert Thong makes a presentation at a medical forum organised by the National University of Singapore: "It is an honour and privilege for me to stand before so distinguished a gathering..."

Late morning, making a phone call home to his wife: "Hi, darl, can't make it for tonight's dinner with the Sims. Sorry. Hey, what's that you said? No, for goodness' sake. I can't do that! No, lah, no can do!"

In the afternoon, on the way to the car park, meeting an acquaintance Dr Arnold Evans from the UK, head of the delegation to the medical forum: "Good afternoon, Dr Evans. It was good that you could make it for the forum. I understand that you had some problems with your flight?"

At the car park, talking to one of the car park attendants: "Hey, there's a scratch on my car! You saw or not, a big scratch. How come you never notice. You car park attendant, you never do your work, or what?"

To his Filipino maid, at home, after dinner: "That mutton dish was very good. You say its name is — what? Special Philippine dish, you say? Maybe next time not so much salt."

Singlish? Dr John Thong and his supporters frown and say, "Certainly not! How disgusting!" But Dr Robert Thong, to annoy his brother, deliberately uses the offensive language in response: "*Aiyah,* okay, *lah,* I tell you!"

Needless to say, I am obliged to take sides in the quarrel.

The Price That Was Paid

Looking back, I think I once paid a high price — a very high one indeed — for being an early devotee of the English language. I was then only twelve. Thrown into an adult world that I did not fully understand, I understood it enough to realise that too much enthusiasm for a foreign language which the adults found difficult to learn, could be construed as intolerable arrogance of the young.

In my early school years, my love of the English language was enough to make me respond enthusiastically to any form of English language teaching, no matter how uninspiring the teacher, or how uninspired the method used. I even enjoyed the 'dictation exercise', possibly the best example of the least effective methodology for language teaching. Using that method, the English language teacher first selected part of a passage from a textbook, then dictated it to us, a short phrase at a time, for us to write it down in our copy books. Ideally, our written product should perfectly match its source.

The dictation exercise, which was then an invariable part of every teacher's repertoire, claimed many benefits for us students. It supposedly made us develop the important listening skill, it allowed us to model our speech on our teacher's correct pronunciation of English words, it enabled us to spell those words correctly and, lastly, it trained us in correct punctuation since, by paying careful attention to the pauses and inflections in the teacher's voice, we would know where to put the commas and full stops and question marks.

All these claims vanished with the arrival of a young teacher, a temporary replacement for our regular English language teacher who had given birth and gone on long leave. For she not only mispronounced many English words, but was abysmally ignorant of the patterns of intonation or rhythm of English speech.

Her voice rose and fell randomly, jumbling up declarative and interrogative sentences, so that we wondered why the hero adventurer of the story she was dictating, who was supposed to be the most alert and curious visitor in a strange land, never asked any questions. She dictated an exclamatory sentence such as 'What treasures he found! How absolutely thrilled he was!' in the flat tones of someone reading out a groceries shopping list.

In addition to dictation, Teacher was given the task of reading stories to us during the 'Storytime' period. She read the most exciting part of an adventure tale, whether it was the hero's victory over the villain or his rescue of a whole village, in a monotone that failed to indicate the story's climax that we were all waiting for, ready to respond with claps and cheers. Instead, as we sat in a circle around this dullest of dull story-reading teachers, we looked at each other wonderingly and realised that the story had come to an end only when she closed her book, stood up and said, "Alright, you may all go back to your places now."

Having fully initiated myself into the wonders of story reading and storytelling from a young age, I was dismayed that such a marvellous human activity could be so dreadfully mismanaged. One day, when the teacher had to interrupt her reading to leave the classroom for a while, I, ever the self-appointed raconteur, boldly went up to her seat, picked up the book she had left there, and began reading it aloud to my classmates. I took care to pronounce loudly and correctly those words she had mispronounced and to read the most exciting part with much theatrical declamation and gesturing. My classmates giggled with delight. I was still enjoying the posturing and the attention when Teacher returned.

Without knowing the full extent of my brazenness in making fun not only of an adult but a teacher, she suspected enough to dislike me intensely from that day onwards. She looked for the earliest opportunity to inflict a punishment severe enough to cure me of my arrogance. It came a few days later, with the dictation exercise.

As she entered the classroom, she eyed me warily, then chose to ignore me completely as she gave the class certain instructions regarding that day's exercise. Since it would be based on a rather difficult passage, we would be given about ten minutes in advance to acquaint ourselves with the 'big' words there, such as 'adventure', 'mischievous', 'relatives', 'celebrate'.

While my classmates screwed their eyes and moved their lips in a determined effort to deal with this daunting passage, I instantly recognised it as part of a story I had previously read and enjoyed. Indeed, I had liked it so much that I knew it by heart. Long sentences in English containing multisyllabic words which I found particularly appealing, often scrolled across my mind. The words were not in clunky block letters but in beautiful flowing script, like that of magnificently illustrated medieval manuscripts.

So, with an easy, nonchalant superiority, I shut my book, pushed it aside and wrote the entire passage from effortless memory on my dictation copy book, finishing it in a fraction of the time given. I spent the rest of the time watching, with smiling patronage, my classmates still in the throes of struggling to memorise the 'big' words.

Then Teacher returned for the dictation exercise. I was nonplussed, suddenly realising the stupidity of what I had done. The exercise would be redundant for me now, since I had already got the whole passage written down, and impeccably too. What was I to do? Should I tell Teacher? I decided to go along with the rest of the class, getting ready for the dictation exercise, with a great pretence of enthusiasm in bringing out my copy book and pencil. As Teacher dictated, I covered the already written passage with my left hand, and with my right, used the pencil to trace, very lightly, each written phrase, in perfect synchronisation with Teacher's dictation, assuming total absorption in the task.

Suddenly Teacher swooped upon me, picked up my copy book, saw the fully pre-copied passage there, and screamed, "How dare you! You are a cheat!" The punishment that followed was swift and methodical. I tried to explain, but my words, in my terror, came out incoherently, and were swamped out by her fury. In any case, she was in no mood to listen to me, the proven mischief maker. She wrote the word 'Cheat' in my copy book, in large angry letters across the ignominious passage. Then she pinned the book to my dress. Next she grabbed my arm and led me out of the classroom, into an open area unshielded from the afternoon sun. "Stand here," she said grimly and went back to the classroom.

But the humiliation was not over.

A teacher from another class who was the school's moral instructor, thought the incident would provide useful moral capital. She brought me in from the sun, and presented me to her class as an example of dishonesty which she said coloured the conscience black. Then she wrote a note, pinned it near the first one, and told me to go back to my class, to show it to my teacher. "Make sure you stand where everybody can see it," she said severely. It was an apology which she had written on my behalf: "I am very sorry for being such a cheat. I am very ashamed of myself. Please forgive me. I will never do such a thing again."

The incident, in its many aspects, overwhelmed me, throwing me into a maelstrom of feelings I couldn't even begin to describe. I remember that in my confusion, agitation, distress and most of all, awareness of cruel injustice, I was unable to cry, which would have brought relief. Instead I could only make small, stupid blubbering sounds. In the strangest way, only one thought stood out with clarity: In future, I must not show off my good English. Otherwise, it would get me into trouble again.

I kept this promise to myself over the years in school. Never again did I conspicuously offer to teach a classmate how to read properly, or correct her homework before she handed it up. For the first time, I was beginning to see my English language competence as a disadvantage that had to be managed, not a gift to be celebrated.

Fortunately, my old affinity with the language had not been lost. Now, more than ever, I regard it as a friend, a confidante, an unfailing ally, a source of deepest pleasure. Its companionship was in the school textbooks that I read avidly, the storybooks that I managed to borrow from the school's small library, the 'Film Fun' comics that my eldest sister who worked as a nurse in another town, sometimes brought home. Indeed I relished all printed material that I could lay my hands on (including some of my father's unreadable accountancy books), as long as they were in English.

Together, I and the language that I would claim as my mother tongue formed a most amiable pair, moving forward in a sweet bonding of companionship, trust and joy. If I could personify English then, it would be as a very kindly parent, ready to indulge me in every way.

The practical outcome of this bonding was that by the time I went into secondary school at the age of twelve, I had achieved mastery of the English language. I spoke it exclusively. I was well ahead not only of my classmates, but of schoolmates at much higher levels. Indeed, it resulted in one teacher, a Mrs Lai, effectively appointing me a co-teacher. She slyly co-opted my help in the marking of the piles of exercise books she seemed always to be burdened with. "There's no need to tell anybody," she said conspiratorially. Of course I never would, as I rather enjoyed the secret honour of being trusted enough to identify, and then correct, the many grammatical and spelling mistakes in the workbooks of students older than myself.

I spent many happy afternoons after school as Mrs Lai's trusted deputy. I loved the feel of the red pencil in my hand, which I used liberally, following Mrs Lai's instructions, to circle the mistakes in the exercise books, and write next to them the abbreviations that helpfully specified their category — 'sp' for spelling, 'gr' for grammar and 'pn' for punctuation. I was filled with pride when I surreptitiously watched my classmates looking shamefaced at the red-marked mistakes in their exercise books when these were returned to them by Mrs Lai. I almost wanted to shout out to them, "Hey, it was I who wrote all that!"

Mrs Lai gave me a dictionary as a reward, which I consulted daily to take my already substantial vocabulary to an even higher level. I told myself I would learn at least ten new words a day. It didn't matter if I would never have the opportunity to use 'penultimate' or 'contemplation' or 'prognostication' or 'contemporary'. The sheer pleasure of their acquaintance was enough, as, having a mystique all their own, they occupied a special place in both my vocabulary notebook and my mind, giving me a secret pleasure I would not share with anyone. If I could personify the English language then, it would be as a romantic partner, ready to please me in every way.

Mrs Lai often boasted to the principal of the school, Sister St Aloysius, that I was her best student, indeed, the school's best student. Sister one day pulled me aside and said in a severe voice matching the serious expression on her face, "You must not be too proud. Jesus does not like proud people. You must try to help your friends instead."

I was not aware that I was being proud, but Sister could not be wrong. So I looked down in shame. In those days I was full of piety and would never do anything to offend Jesus, or the rest of the Holy Family, including his mother Mary, his earthly father Joseph and, by extension, Mary's holy parents Joachim and Anna, all of whom I knew and loved from the stories that I heard in the catechism classes. I decided that I would never ever show off my English again.

It was through Sister St Aloysius that I had to pay the price once again, at the age of twelve, for my strong attachment to the language. And this time, the price was so high and so crushing to my spirit, that I believe its effect remains to this day.

It is a complex story which needs some simplification in the telling. It involved mainly a new student called Theresa who had just been enrolled in the school. Her mother was apparently a good friend of Sister St Aloysius, not least because she had converted to the Catholic religion and induced her entire family, comprising her husband, two sons and three daughters, to do likewise. She chose for them the names of illustrious saints such as Ignatius, Benedict and Gregory, Seraphina, Philomena and Theresa.

The other reason for her closeness with Sister St Aloysius was her wealth which had enabled her to pay for a large and beautiful shrine to the Virgin Mary, set up on the grounds of Sister's convent school.

My part in the story had to do with only two stark facts: Firstly, that Theresa, the brightest in the family, was her mother's favourite child; and secondly, that the mother's dearest wish was for Theresa to be selected to represent not only her school but all the schools in the state, in a prestigious statewide English essay competition that would surely be reported in the newspapers.

The trouble was that I stood in the way. I was seen as a threat because I was capable of submitting a much better essay in the competition and thus easily beating Theresa to the championship. That was an unthinkable prospect to her mother, and, by extension, to Sister St Aloysius, the two women being now inextricably locked in a mutual dependency of understanding, need and trust. So, in one stroke, I had become not only Theresa's rival but Sister's foe.

Sister never did anything by halves. Her initial antipathy towards me burgeoned into a full-blown hatred, only matched by the magnitude of her loyalty to Theresa's mother. She had to do something to remove me as the doubly hateful opponent. Fiercely single-minded in the pursuit of her goals, she quickly found the best way to do it. It would be through religion, since she understood its power best.

She pulled me aside one afternoon and said to me in a grave voice, "To prove your love for Jesus, make a sacrifice. A small sacrifice compared to the great one He made for us." And then she explained what the sacrifice should be: "You will not take part in the essay competition. I will inform the organisers."

In a single utterance, she had applied the highest religious theology to the meanest of worldly initiatives.

I did not fully understand what she meant, but immediately grasped the central message: I would no longer be taking part in an essay competition that I had been looking forward to. I stared at her, but was too shocked to say anything. In any case, students never talked back to their teachers, much less to a school principal.

To my secret relief, I found out, from what I could gather from the confusing mix of events that followed, that Mrs Lai had already long since submitted my name for the competition (as well as Theresa's, upon Sister's insistence) to the organisers. Submission was a formal procedure, requiring proper registration. For the school to withdraw my candidature for no real reason could result in a barrage of puzzled questions not only from Mrs Lai but other teachers, that Sister would have no stomach for. She had to think of another strategy. Still pursuing the religious angle, she hit upon a second and even more ingenious strategy, one that she knew would strike me at the deepest core of my fears — the fear of hell.

I recollect vividly now, even after so many years, the careful orchestration of Sister's game plan. She started with the most basic level, by informing me of a sin which I might not suspect I had. She told me that she had noticed the sin of pride in me. I began to cry, frightened at the thought of being a sinful person. Assured by my fear, she went on to the next step of reinforcing it. "Do you know," she said ominously, "that pride is one of the Seven Deadly Sins?" She mentioned the other six, but stressed that pride was the greatest because it had caused the fall of the great Archangel Michael himself. Then she ingeniously suggested how I could get rid of this mortal sin:

"When you write your essay in the competition hall, make it such that it will not win you a prize. For that will increase your pride."

Her suggestion was just too costly! I couldn't pay such a price. I stared at Sister, distress written all over my face. She ignored the distress, as it had become entirely irrelevant in her determination to hasten her grand plan for securing victory for Theresa. In the clearest of tones and the most specific of instructions, she told me how I could get rid of my sinful pride:

"Make as many mistakes as possible in your essay. Write sentences with grammar and spelling mistakes. Use the wrong words. Don't bother with proper paragraphing or correct punctuation."

It was the strangest advice I had ever heard, the exact reverse of what every conscientious English language teacher regularly gave her students. I prided myself on the compositions I wrote for my teachers, which I made sure were really good, indeed so good that Mrs Lai would sometimes get me to read them out to the class, making me glow with pride. What, do the opposite? Make grammar mistakes? Write bad sentences which would sound downright nonsensical? Use the wrong words when I had always been meticulously using only the right ones, having diligently, painstakingly compiled lists of words with the full range of their nuances and subtleties in meaning? Spell words wrongly when I would check, with untiring zeal, for their correct spelling in the dictionary that Mrs Lai had given me?

It was hard for me to see the connection between this need to abuse the English language, and my love for Jesus. So I stared even harder at Sister. She gave a small sigh of weariness as she took pains to explain to me the logical connections between her various propositions:

"Your pride will increase if you get the Essay Competition prize. So you must make sure not to get the prize, in order not to displease Jesus. You can only do this if you make as many mistakes as possible in your essay. This sacrifice may bring some pain, but it is worth it, because it will please Jesus. Remember the sacrifice He made for love of you? Your pain cannot be compared to his. See?"

I could not see. Sister saw the continuing bewilderment on my face. Now was the moment, in a climax of malicious purpose, to deliver the coup de grâce that would, once and for all, devastate me and put me completely in her power:

"You will go to hell if you do not get rid of your mortal sin of pride."

As she expected, my bewilderment was suddenly replaced by sheer terror. Sister knew she had got me at last. She looked at me with the bright-eyed satisfaction of the ultimate, hard-won victory.

At the age of twelve, my image of hell, created by the many fearsome descriptions in the catechism classes, and helped by my overactive imagination, was of a terrifying abyss of fire and brimstone where sinful people suffered excruciatingly for their sins. The gluttons would always be hungry and thirsty, reaching out for food and water that were mere hallucinations. The adulterers would have their naked bodies dipped in boiling oil. The greedy and covetous would be suffocated with bags of money on their chests and heavy pouches of gold coins hanging from their necks, making them unable to breathe. I visualised the punishment in hell for proud people like me. We would have our minds depleted of all thinking power, so that they would be like empty vessels making a lot of noise as we were led around on a leash, followed by jeering crowds.

And all this would be for eternity. I tried to picture eternity with the help of an analogy I had once heard in a fiery sermon by a priest. Imagine a huge rock. Every thousand years, a little bird flies by, and pecks the rock with its tiny beak. Eternity is when the little bird has completely worn down the rock.

The total impact of the years of secret terrors came crashing upon me. I broke down in tears and told Sister that I didn't want to go to hell. "Then you know what to do," she said matter-of-factly. "It is entirely up to you to decide how to write your essay in the competition hall."

To make sure that I remained in thrall to the threat of hellfire right throughout my writing of the competition essay, Sister had actually volunteered to be one of the invigilators in the hall, convinced that her physical presence would be a deterrent to any sudden return to my previous status as the dedicated English language standard bearer. That to her would be something absolutely out of the question.

Walking slowly between the rows of desks where the competitors sat writing with intense concentration, Sister and her fellow invigilators did their work of making sure there was no cheating and no undue disturbance of the perfect silence in the competition hall. At suitable intervals, they raised their voices to announce to the candidates, "Half an hour more", "Fifteen minutes more", "Time to stop", finally collecting the finished scripts and making sure the candidates left the hall in an orderly manner.

Clearly Sister was only concerned with one precise duty in her role that day: to remind me of my promise to produce an essay unfit for any competition. She would pause a little when she passed my desk, and give me a sharp, knowing look that said, "Make as many mistakes as possible. Remember what I said." It was the most surreal situation imaginable, an educationist urging a good student, under pain of punishment of hell itself, to go against her strongest instincts for excellence and success.

Sister's unstoppable, passionate commitment to get me out of Theresa's way, had taken on the sinister, dark aspect of an obsession. Even her eyes, as she looked at me, had the concentrated ferocity of deranged purpose. Till this very day, I cannot explain how a person dedicated to the calm, contemplative life of nuns could have become so horribly embroiled in the murky affairs of the world outside the convent walls. Today's psychologists would probably explain Sister's behaviour in terms of some serious personality disorder such as schizophrenia which was all the more exacerbated by the strictness of a nun's life. It needed to explode at some point and I was unfortunate enough to be in the way of the explosion.

So, did I obey Sister's injunction? Did I, for the sake of my well-being in the next world, mess up my efforts in this? Alas, I did. In that hour in the hall, I was completely under an influence that locked up all my powers of thinking, reasoning and feeling. I was like the hypnotic bound to the hypnotist, the bewitched bound to the sorcerer. Never underestimate the hold that a hysterically delusional authority figure, driven by a combination of secular and religious power, can have on a terrified child of twelve.

Of that traumatic day of the competition, I only remember an overwhelming feeling of nausea as I sat at my desk, unable to write beyond a single paragraph, probably one that didn't make sense, with its words swimming before my eyes. I also remember Sister going round with the other invigilators, at the end of the allotted time, to pick up the candidates' scripts. She stopped at my desk to pick up mine, saw the haphazardly written single paragraph and gave a pleased smile. That very day she must have called Theresa's mother to assure her that everything would go smoothly for her daughter.

That horrifying experience, more than six decades ago, has not exactly receded into the mists of memory. A day after the competition, I fell ill and was confined to bed for a week. I suffered nightmares in which Mrs Lai scolded me for my poor grades and threatened to take back the dictionary. In one of the dreams, I had a sheet of paper, containing that one shameful single paragraph that was supposedly my best effort for a prestigious statewide competition, pinned to my blouse as I stood in front of a public building somewhere along the main road of my little town. I was surrounded by jeering onlookers, among whom stood a disappointed Mrs Lai looking tearfully at me. My mother attributed my illness to the stress of oncoming puberty. I am more inclined to think it had to do with possibly the greatest trauma of my young life.

Fortunately, the English language and I, estranged for a while by an episode too twisted and warped to comprehend, are once more the best of friends and companions, devoted supporters of each other.

I don't know what happened to Theresa, or whether she won the state prize in the competition. Many years later, when I heard that Sister St Aloysius, in her old age, had dementia and was cruelly crippled with arthritis, I decided to pay her a visit. She was bent double, the loose nun's habit unable to hide the skeletal frame under it, the nun's coif almost falling over a hollowed-out face. She was a totally unrecognisable version of the stout, energetic, incredibly mobile Sister St Aloysius I knew.

I stood before her and gently greeted her. Then something extraordinary happened. Her dementia-clogged mind unclogged for one brilliant moment of perfect recollection as soon as she saw and recognised me. She held my hand and, with tears in her eyes, spoke of the Theresa incident so many years ago. "You made the most noble sacrifice," she said quaveringly. "You did God's work. God bless you." I could only say silently, in a surge of rage that almost overcame the compassion: "Because of you, Sister, 'sacrifice' has become the most toxic word in my vocabulary. I have never used it since."

I remember the day when I had picked up a red pencil and savagely scratched out the word from the dictionary that Mrs Lai had given me, which I still have, incredibly, after so many years.

Lost (Delightfully) in Translation

My little hometown Kulim could actually lay claim to a place in the history of peninsular Malaysia (then called Malaya) because it was the battleground of a guerrilla war being waged by the country against its Communist foes. The war, called the Malayan Emergency, which lasted between 1948 and 1960, ended with a resounding victory for the country, that would not have been possible without the strong support of the British military.

We sometimes saw the dead bodies of the enemies brought out from their hiding places deep in the jungle, and exhibited in the town's open marketplace, as a stern warning to all. Malayan and British soldiers would stand guard, suspiciously scanning the faces of those who came to watch, as if these were secret Communist sympathisers. One day — I must have been about ten years old — I accompanied a maidservant who was eager to see one of these bodies, laid out on the ground. We stood among the circle of onlookers gazing silently, gravely at it. The corpse with its close cropped hair and rough khaki trousers and shirt, looked to be male.

Suddenly a young British officer, wearing heavy army boots, raised his right foot and held it over the dead body. I gave a little scream, thinking the rather brutal-looking soldier was going to stomp on the corpse. But no. With an arrogant smile, he used his heavy-booted foot to flip over the corpse's unbuttoned shirt, exposing a woman's bare breast, bloodied by bullets. There was a collective gasp from the crowd.

Years later, as a writer, I wanted to write about this poor woman, perhaps weave a tragically romantic story about a kampong girl who had to leave home and the young man she was engaged to marry, after she was forcibly recruited by the Communists. I would write about her being trained to use a rifle, roughly told to get used to the mosquitoes, snakes and scorpions in the jungle, ordered to join some of her now fellow fighters hiding in the dense jungle undergrowth to mount an ambush on a patrol of the hated British soldiers.

One day she was shot and killed by the very man she had been betrothed to. For, in a supreme twist of irony, he was among those who had been recruited by the opposite side and trained to become a very effective combatant. He recognised her only by the small silver pendant that he had given her, years back, as a mark of their betrothal, which she wore on a chain around her neck. (The crucial role of small personal items such as a ring or pendant, given at birth or as tokens of remembrance, as the surest means for identification, followed by emotional reunion, was an absolute must in my early attempts at story writing.)

But I never managed to write the story about the dead

woman with the bullet-riddled breast. Perhaps it was too painful for me. Indeed, there were many incidents that I had heard from adults which stayed in my memory for years, unable to come to life through my pen.

There was one incident from the Emergency, however, which I had not only written about, but also referred to freely and enthusiastically in my lectures. It had nothing to do with the terrors of war, and everything, oddly, to do with the pleasures afforded by the richness of the English language.

It involved a very unlikely person, who used the language mainly for shouting orders and angry expletives at incompetent subordinates. He was a general named Sir Gerald Templer, one of the best known and most respected figures of the war against the Communists. Indeed, some historians were ready to aver that he single-handedly won that war.

Sir Gerald was a driven man, relentless and ruthless in his goal to destroy the enemy. One of his methods was collective punishment of the enemy's sympathisers. If he even remotely suspected a single individual in a village of helping the Communists, such as by smuggling food or medicine into the jungle for them, he would punish the entire village. His shrewd understanding of the strong Chinese tradition of communal purpose and consensual action helped him achieve his aims.

One day he heard that someone from a certain village, situated on the edge of the jungle, was spying for the Communists. Immediately he called for his helicopter, descended upon that village, and summoned the headman to gather all the villagers around him. Standing in the centre, he surveyed them with cold hostility. With him was a translator.

Looking at them sternly with his steely blue eyes, Sir Gerald began by saying, "You bastards." He turned to the translator who said in Hokkien to the villagers, "His Excellency says that your fathers and mothers were not married." The villagers responded with puzzled looks, but did not dare turn to exchange frowns with each other, maintaining their impassive expressions. Sir Gerald went on with grim warning, "You may be bastards, but I'll prove a bigger bastard!" The translator intoned, "His Excellency says that his parents too were not married." By then it was impossible for the villagers to hold back their puzzlement. They broke out in excited chatter among themselves, asking questions of each other, but chiefly smiling broad smiles of relief, since the tension had resolved in harmless anticlimax.

This incident may be purely apocryphal, but I love it for its wonderful illustration of the double meanings of so many English words which seemed deliberately designed to create a hilarious breakdown in communication. The system of denotation and connotation in the use of English words favours this breakdown: The good general had used 'bastard' with its powerful connotations of infamy, notoriety and social ignominy, getting all worked up, while the translator stuck to its purely denotative, literal meaning, remaining calm and expressionless. I must have been thinking of this translator when I penned this little verse:

The Chinese translator pored over
'Out of sight, out of mind'.
He thought long and at last wrote
'An idiot who is also blind'.

I have a collection of actual lost-in-translation jokes, shared all over the world by dedicated humorists (who must have longer-than-average life expectancies, since laughter is supposed to be life enhancing).

Several involve the verb 'bear' which belies its simplicity by being fraught with all kinds of connotations unknown to the inexperienced non-native speaker. Witness the sign put up in a hotel lobby in Bucharest which reads: 'The lift is being fixed for the next day. During that time, we regret that you will be unbearable.'

I'm also thinking of that poor Indian guy who ambitiously tried to enlarge his English vocabulary by making it a practice when using an English word to do so with its full range of synonyms. When he was told by the doctor that his wife was unable to have children, he sadly informed his relatives thus: "My wife is unbearable, inconceivable and impregnable."

There is a plethora of English words that must be the bane of learners for they sound alike, are spelt almost identically and yet have completely different meanings: 'lose' and 'loose', 'affect' and 'effect', 'diseased' and 'deceased', 'compliment' and 'complement', 'elicit' and 'illicit'. Students often confuse one with the other, sometimes unintentionally producing sentences that can be so memorably comical that they have created a special genre of humour called Student Howlers.

When I was a teacher of English in a secondary school, I used to collect these howlers to share with my colleagues. My favourite was by a student who wrote with pride about the many achievements of the Singapore leaders, ending with the sentence: "We are a rich country with a high standard of living, and high moral standards. We are a truly effluent society under the PAP government."

Other favourites: "Francis Drake circumcised the world with a hundred-foot clipper." "We presented the Inspector with a plague inscribed with the school motto." "People were very worried since they believed that war was eminent." "The soil here is very fertile because it is full of micro-orgasms."

I was teaching English in a lower secondary class, where the students were about thirteen or fourteen years old, when I had an idea which I thought might cure some students of their habit of misspelling words and producing howlers as a result. "The hunter fired shorts into the air." "Those who come late to school will be canned by the Discipline Master." "It was a rainy day and my bicycle rode through a lot of poodles." I thought that getting those misspellers to come up to the blackboard and illustrate their misspelt sentences might both startle and amuse them into curing themselves permanently of their bad habit.

At first they came up hesitantly but soon got so much into the spirit and fun of the exercise that the lesson descended into pure classroom mayhem. Excitedly and very noisily, they competed with each other to produce the best graphics, some revealing for the first time, their considerable talent as cartoonists and caricaturists.

The noise caused the Discipline Master to investigate. His nickname among the students was 'Botak', a rude reference to his baldness, and he certainly wasn't amused by the picture on the blackboard showing a man with a completely bald head stuffing a struggling student into a large sardine can. He looked with frowning suspicion at the other two drawings, and probably wondered if the picture of three identical pairs of the school shorts obscenely shooting out into the air from a large gun barrel, and of a bicycle cruelly ploughing through small, curly-haired dogs, were also making fun of him.

I wonder how the student of the 'effluent society' howler would have illustrated it.

English idioms are fiendishly difficult to use correctly, and are best avoided by the learner, if simple, direct and literal expressions can be used instead. There was a tale making the rounds, about the young wife of a Pakistani diplomat, newly arrived in London, with an eagerness to start learning the language properly. She must have spent hours practising proper greetings, salutations and social pleasantries. One day, she and her husband gave a party at which she was keen to practise her English, determined to move beyond simple, direct expressions to the more sophisticated idioms. She had no idea about the linguistic minefield she was entering.

When one of the guests presented her with a gift, instead of simply saying, "Thank you very much", thereby circumventing the dangerous mines, she said, with self-conscious effort, "I thank you from the heart of my bottom." That part of her anatomy was particularly pronounced, and two women among the guests later confessed to sneaking out into the garden where they held on to each other in hysterical laughter. Any English idiom containing 'bottom', 'backside', 'butt', 'rump', 'chest' or 'balls' should be assiduously avoided by non-native speakers.

It was said that the Pakistan diplomat's wife made things worse later in the evening when she wanted to join the other wives who were making teasing remarks about their husbands. One said hers was a stick-in-the-mud, while another wished that hers, a perpetual dawdler, would strike while the iron was hot. Somehow the idiom was the favoured mode for spousal raillery.

Our brave learner had previously learnt an English idiom, among many others, which she thought would apply suitably to her husband who liked to busy himself with other people's concerns. She had said laughingly to him, as she looked up from her book of English idioms, "Ah, you have a finger in every pie!" But she could not recollect the idiom at the party, being only vaguely aware that it was about having a finger in some western food. So she exclaimed brightly, pointing to her husband, "Yes, my husband is very bad. He has a finger in every tart!"

The double meanings of words, their layered connotations, the sly allusions, the eccentricity of idioms, the sheer quagmire that the English language can cause the unwary learner to flounder and splutter in, must make it the humorist's best friend. If I could personify English here, it would be as the court jester, the joker and the prankster, leaving a trail of exasperation and delight, in equal measure.

English Grammar
Inspires a Tale

As an English language teacher, I had found it extremely difficult to teach a certain feature of English grammar called the Subjunctive Mood, illustrated in 'If' sentences: 'If he had known, he wouldn't have done such a thing.' 'If the assassin's bullet had missed, World War I would not have started.' 'If only I could turn back the clock!' But as a writer, I found it very useful, since it was the mode for expressing the wide range of emotions — regret, doubt, disillusionment and frustration — that I often explored in my stories.

The Subjunctive Mood inspired the following tale.

Sitting in the school staffroom, marking the written compositions of her students, Miss Sundram was an oasis of calm and tranquillity amidst the hubbub around her — the loud voices of her colleagues, shrill with laughter or complaint, the scraping sound of chairs being dragged out from under the staffroom table, the thudding sound of stacks of student exercise books heavily, wearily plonked upon the staff table.

"Miss Sundram, there's a call for you." Miss Sundram often received calls on the one telephone made available to the staff,

discreetly placed on a table in a far corner of the staffroom, behind a screen. Nobody thought to call her 'Lalitha', even though she had been a colleague for years and had always been friendly and helpful; the formality of address suited her quiet demeanour and preferred solitude.

Even her students approached her formally. But they enjoyed her lessons. They said she explained English grammar in a way that they could easily understand, gave them much useful practice in its correct usage, and was always thinking of new ways of helping them. Without being able to use such words as 'inventive' or 'committed' or 'unstinting', they were praising her in exactly those terms.

They said they learnt to use the Past Tense form correctly through a clever teaching method that Miss Sundram used. First she got them to think of past examples of enjoyable family and other incidents which they remembered well. Next she made them voice out those examples, which they did readily enough: "Last holidays my father he rent a bungalow and we all enjoy ourselves very much." "Yesterday my sister celebrate her birthday with many presents." "One day, at the market, I mistake somebody for my best friend."

Miss Sundram wrote those sentences on the board exactly as they had been uttered, and painstakingly explained each mistake. Then she got the students to go up to the blackboard to rewrite the sentences correctly. Finally she asked them to read out the corrected sentences slowly. "Don't they sound so much better now?" she said encouragingly. And indeed they did.

The school principal, Mrs Tang, liked Miss Sundram enough to disregard the nickname that her colleagues had given her — 'The Mystery Woman'. Mrs Tang said with a frown, "What if she never reveals anything about herself or her background? That is entirely her business. Don't be such busybodies!"

The only thing they knew about her was that she had an elderly father as she often got telephone calls from him, and the only thing they knew about him was that he was aged eighty and not in good health, the information gathered from bits of conversation overheard by the insatiably curious Mrs Ong. Mrs Ong's solicitous inquiries about her father's health had elicited no more than the invariably polite, "Yes, he's well, thank you", from Miss Sundram.

Mrs Ong would have been exasperated by the determined unresponsiveness of Miss Sundram, if the latter had not shown exactly the opposite when approached for help in matters related to the intricacies of English grammar. Miss Sundram was the acknowledged expert, and she shared her knowledge freely and generously. She was ready to come out of her isolation to answer any question on the subject, and just as ready to slip back into it once her help had been given.

Her colleagues sought her assistance endlessly, sometimes out of genuine need, often out of sheer laziness. Instead of making the effort to check on rules of usage in a grammar text, or the precise meaning of a word in the dictionary, they found it so much easier to turn to Miss Sundram, as she sat marking exercise books or preparing notes for the next day's lesson, and simply say with a friendly, half-apologetic laugh, "Excuse me, Miss Sundram. I've got to kachau you once again!"

"Our Miss Sundram is a gem," enthused Mrs Ong, and in the same breath whispered to the equally inquisitive Miss Rodrigues, "but why is she such a mystery? The other day, she received no less than four calls from her father. Doesn't she have any siblings to help take care of him? Somebody once said she has a married sister who's now living in the UK."

"It's unusual for Indian women to remain unmarried. How old is Miss Sundram now? Late thirties?"

"Maybe she feels it's her duty to take care of the old, sickly father."

"But surely she would want to get married and have a home and family of her own?"

One day the school had a new staff member, a young teacher named Rajeswari Joseph who would turn Miss Sundram's world upside down. Miss Joseph, who insisted on being called Wari, had just got married and could not stop talking about her husband, their honeymoon, their lives together, with the unabashed extravagance of the pure extrovert, all the time playing with an abundance of curls that fell licentiously on her bare shoulders.

She chortled, "You know, my Francis pounces on me and says, 'Ah, my Wari, you mustn't be wary of your dear hubby!'" and made much of the ingenuity of her pun.

Miss Sundram winced, but only imperceptibly. Mrs Ong and Miss Rodrigues looked at each other with knowing smiles, their prurience prompting them to encourage Wari to go on talking.

A few days later, the newcomer suddenly pulled Miss Sundram aside and said in excited whispers, "Hey, how come when I mentioned my husband's name — Francis Dhillon — you never said anything? He says you know each other! He met you years back. In fact he was in love with you. Imagine that! Is it true? How cute!" The information, questions, exclamations and comments all tumbled out in a *breathless heap. Wari eagerly grasped Miss Sundram's hands in readiness for an enjoyable sharing of intimacies.*

Yes, it was true. But it was far from cute. It was a tragic tale of lost love and lost happiness. Francis Dhillon had ardently courted her for a year. She had never been happier. At last he proposed. Her father said 'No' resolutely. Miss Sundram pleaded, reminding him that he had readily given permission for her younger sister to marry; moreover, the sister's partner was someone from a different race. But the father had merely grunted, "She's different", and Miss Sundram had thought with a bitterness she would not have dared to express directly, "Yes, different from me. Different enough to stand up to you. She'll never devote her life to taking care of you."

Francis Dhillon had left in disappointment and sorrow. His last words to her were seared into her very being: "I'll wait for you." But she never heard from him again. Someone told her he had gone to live in Malaysia.

Wari was one of those females whose enjoyment of victory was all the greater when it had been snatched, completely and dramatically, from a close rival who should thereafter never recover from her loss. Even as a rival now safely consigned to defeat, Miss Sundram, with her calm air, exhibited an exasperating superiority that was simply intolerable. Wari wanted to see the calmness collapse in a devastation of bitter tears or at least darken with profound envy. But there was nothing that she could say about Francis Dhillon — not even his expert love-making — that could cause any change of expression on that imperturbable face.

"What are you doing, Lalitha?" the irrepressible Wari leaned over to look at what Miss Sundram was writing on a sheet of paper. She read out loudly, "Subjunctive Mood.

Whatever's that? I never learnt that in school!" Miss Sundram said quietly, without looking up, "It's part of English grammar. I'll be teaching it afterwards."

Wari said archly, "Francis told me that he used to call you 'Litha', his pet name for you. He told me so much about you. Why did you give him up? You know, it broke his heart. Luckily he's now able to say to me, 'But you mended it', and follow that up with you-know-what." She gave a coarse wink followed by a little shriek of laughter. Carried along on an unstoppable stream of malice, she continued, "I once asked him whether he had made love to you, but he wouldn't tell me! I insisted, promising not to be jealous, and he said, no, he respected you too much to do what would have made you uncomfortable. But he told me you allowed him to kiss you. Did you? No need to be shy, lah! Let's compare notes. Don't you think he's a great kisser?"

Miss Sundram excused herself to go to the washroom where she stood before the mirror, staring at herself and the tears of rage forming in her eyes. She stared for some time. Then brushing them off quickly, she got ready to go for her lesson on the Subjunctive Mood.

As soon as she entered the classroom, the students sensed that something was wrong. Her eyes had the uncannily bright look of impending self-destruction. She wrote 'Subjunctive Mood' in large letters on the top of the blackboard, and turned to face the class, her countenance ashen white. "Let me give you examples of the Subjunctive Mood," she said in a constricted, hardly audible voice. But the voice quickly swelled in a rampage of loud screaming. "If only I had been brave enough to stand up to that bully! If I had listened to my heart, I wouldn't be so miserable today! Now I've lost everything. He'll never come back to me. If only I had spat upon that tyrant and said, 'You call yourself a father? You are the most selfish man on earth!' If only I had told him that to his face! Oh! Oh!"

"You want to know more?" she shrieked at her students. By now, her impeccably coiled hair had uncoiled and fallen in a thick black rope down her back. "If only I had stuck a knife through his selfish heart! If only —"

One of the students ran to get the principal. She arrived in agitated haste to find Miss Sundram sitting on a chair quietly sobbing, surrounded by her students solicitously offering consolation, tissue paper, a cup of hot water.

Cursing in Hokkien, Cursing in English

Curses in English are mild, compared to those in Hokkien which can be so powerful that they could affect you for life. A curse thrown at you as a child would still be reverberating in your ears as an adult, filling you with fear. English curses — 'Go to hell!', 'Damn you', 'Bloody' (a reference to the blood of Jesus) — are derived mainly from Judeo-Christian traditions centred on divine wrath, damnation, lost souls, hellfire and eternal punishment, and through their proliferation in casual speech and literature, have largely lost their impact.

Hokkien curses, however, deal with the most dire of existential issues, that is, death itself, brought about by the most fearsome forces in nature. *May the Lightning God strike you dead. May the Thunder God hurl his thunderbolts at you.* Just as the greatest blessing is to have longevity, the greatest curse is to have life shortened by the mandate of heaven expressed through its violent agents. *Tay Mia. Eow Siew.* These Hokkien curses will strike terror into any heart.

In one of my stories, I dealt with a situation that I had personally witnessed, with great interest. It was the conflict between an elderly, uneducated Hokkien woman and her young, formidable, English-educated daughter-in-law, whom she was forced to live with. "It was my son's decision," she would confide bitterly to her friends. "I had no choice." She could have added, "I have lost my son. That woman's a demon." But she reckoned without her power to curse, backed up by a thousand-year-old tradition.

Among my colleagues in the secondary school where I taught many years ago, there was one — we'll call her Lucy — who would regale us with mother-in-law horror stories, as we sat sipping coffee in the staffroom between lessons. Lucy was one of those very attractive, vibrant women who went about life very efficiently and purposefully, guided by a grand scheme that she had laid out for herself, after much careful and shrewd planning. It was a scheme premised purely on self interest, into which she could fit everything that did not go against that compelling force. The scheme accommodated a very compliant husband; two bright, well-behaved children; a hardworking staff comprising two maidservants, a gardener and a chauffeur. Even the smallest threat to this paradigm of perfection was instantly recognised and repulsed, or rendered harmless, even tamed to become an advantage.

Lucy confessed that the issue of the troublesome mother-in-law took some taming. "But here she is now; she's learnt her lesson, and knows her place," she said triumphantly, adding cheerfully, "We can now laugh at that old pest as much as we like." She wittily nicknamed her mother-in-law 'Mil', not as an abbreviation of her name but as an abbreviation of the idiom for the heaviest possible burden anyone can bear: the millstone round the neck.

"You know what —", Lucy always began her story about her mother-in-law with the three words which had become the summons to whoever was free to gather round her and be ready for at least fifteen minutes of pure fun and laughter. "You know what. Last night Mil threatened to leave," she said, her eyes bright with the thrill of narration. "She actually began to put her things in two large paper bags. Phil was stupid enough to be taken in, but I signalled to him that it was all a bluff. And so it was. Where can she go? Nobody wants to take her in. Years ago, I had agreed to do so, and yet they all think I'm the villainess of the piece!" She rattled off the names of Phil's numerous siblings and their spouses. "You'd think they'd offer something for her upkeep, at least give her some pocket money every month. Nothing of the kind!"

Then she got tired of talking about her mother-in-law, and began to talk about how she was preparing for the birth of her baby, her first after eight years of marriage. "Phil and I are absolutely thrilled. We don't even want to find out the sex of the baby. Boy or girl — it's going to be the same wonderful experience." She confided, with pleased smiles, that her mother, a very traditional Taoist, had gone to consult some temple monks, and brought back a bottle of blessed holy water for her to drink, for the welfare of the child growing inside her.

Lucy said, "At first I resisted, you know, being a Christian. But then I thought, what if my mother is right, and the blessed water is good for my baby. So I drank it. Anything for my baby! But I didn't tell Phil, in case he disapproves. He thinks my mother is all superstitious nonsense!"

Lucy had more to share. Lowering her voice she said, her eyes narrowing with unshakeable purpose, "You know what. After my baby's arrival, I'm going to ask the old fool to leave. Not enough room in the house, with the baby's nanny and all! That will be my excuse. Out she goes. I don't care where she goes, as long as it's out." She spelt out the three-letter word that was beginning to sound very sweet to her ears: "O,U,T."

Suddenly I felt a deep dislike for Lucy. I had a choice: Either walk away and have nothing more to do with her, or write a story about her. I decided on the latter.

In my story, there is a continuing feud between my protagonist (nicknamed Lucifera, Luci for short) and her mother-in-law. Luci is pregnant for the first time and worries that the stress of her mother-in-law's presence will be harmful for her pregnancy. The stress increases when she is told by her maid that the mother-in-law has been spreading tales about her among the neighbours, complaining about her total lack of respect for the old, her utter meanness towards the helpless elderly. Luci is so angry that she breaks into hysterical tears. She screams, "She lives under my roof, she eats my food, and she dares talk that way about me!"

The climax of the story is the confrontation between Luci and her mother-in-law. Unable to speak intelligibly in Hokkien, she resorts to pure English, hoping that the rage in her voice will have the combined force of all the curses offered by the language. The old woman listens silently, then rises to the full height of her powers. With an ancient, powerful tradition behind her, she, in her turn, begins to curse her daughter-in-law. And her curse is all the more effective because she has the backing of the gods: The sin most offensive to them is the sin of filial impiety.

But alas, as a writer writing in English, I found it impossible to capture her curse in its full virulence, steeped in the images of the Lightning God, the Thunder God and the whole pantheon of deities waiting to punish unfilial offspring. Hokkien curses are untranslatable. English curses, even at their most vehement, are no match. So I did the next best thing. It was an awkward device, but it was all I could manage.

This was a strategy sometimes used by writers in English to create an atmosphere of heavy foreboding, to elicit deep awe in the reader. It was the employment of archaic English such as is found in ancient sacred writings, including the Bible. In the exaltation of its tone, and the remoteness of its language, it would strike fear in the reader's heart.

So in my story, the mother-in-law rises magisterially, stands upright, looks straight at her daughter-in-law and cries out: "I curse you! Even though you are with child, I curse you! Heaven's wrath is come to you, because you show no respect for the grey hairs on my head! Henceforth, you and the child in your womb stand accursed in the sight of Almighty God, He who has knowledge of everything under the moon and stars! He strikes with a mighty hand!" And as if to show divine endorsement of the curse, there is the rumble of thunder. Soon a storm breaks out. The old woman rushes out in the pouring rain.

Luci never recovers from the curse. She circles her belly with her arms, in a tight, protective embrace of the child growing inside her. She has bad dreams. In one of them, her child is born without arms; in another, without legs.

She goes to see her priest who prays with her, touching her belly with a crucifix. She goes with her mother to the temple to get more blessed temple water which she rubs on her belly. She consults her doctor who examines her thoroughly and says, "Look, there's nothing wrong with your baby. It's doing fine."

But Luci continues to weep. Her husband Phil decides that there's only one thing to be done. He takes his wife to see his mother who is now staying with one of her daughters.

The old woman turns her face away, refusing to look at her daughter-in-law who stands pleadingly before her. "Please, Mother, please do it for my sake," Phil begs. Very grudgingly she agrees to write something on a sheet of paper that Phil has held out to her. It is a sacred word, recommended by the temple priest, that will negate her curse. The priest says that even the most powerful curse can be undone, if a ceremony is properly conducted.

The story ends with a careful step-by-step carrying out of the ceremony. The piece of paper with the sacred word is held aloft by the priest as he chants out, sonorously, the words of a long-forgotten ritual. The paper is then burnt, to more chanting. The tiny amount of ashes is carefully picked up and dropped into a glass of water which is then presented to Luci. She receives it with both hands, her head bowed in deep respect, and drinks it reverently, gratefully, down to the last drop.

Singapore, for Better or for Verse

As a social and political commentator I had written many articles that, as could be expected, displeased the government, and brought a certain measure of PAP wrath upon my head. The style of these commentaries had been necessarily formal and the tone tendentious, adding to the displeasing effect.

I had asked myself: What if I had used a different mode of criticism? What if I had commented on the stern, controlling PAP leadership and its dislike of dissent, in light-hearted verse instead of the austerely formal, measured prose of the essay? Would the effect be the same?

In a bold experiment, I recruited the help of the quatrain, which is possibly the simplest form of poetry in the English language, consisting only of four lines with optional rhyming patterns. The simplest pattern for me was the ABCB, that is, only the second and fourth lines need to rhyme (unlike the more demanding ABAB or ABBA patterns, for instance). To my relief and delight, I discovered that I could use the quatrain to produce several poems-of-sorts to convey my message, with barely disguised sarcasm, that true political freedom is lacking in Singapore:

The loud activist, the demagogue
In Singapore has no place:
The rabble-rouser with raised fist
Is a pimple on the fair face.

World reports and surveys
Are impressed by Singapore;
They note its glowing charts
And watch its economy soar.

An 'A' for sound investments,
An 'A' for rule of law,
An 'A plus' for governance,
Each is a perfect score.

But it is a dismaying 'D'
For freedom of the press,
Political debate and dissent
Get a grade that's even less.

Encouraged by the ease with which I could use the quatrain, I exploited it further to convey annoyance at the thought that we Singaporeans have ourselves to blame to a great extent for our unquestioning acceptance of PAP dominance:

"We do have freedom," say Singaporeans,
"It's clear from our present status,

Since we are free to do everything
The PAP government lets us."

"Political freedom on a leash?
A tight one, for that matter?
Oh, c'mon, people, do be fair,
The leash is now much longer!

To rant and rage as you like
There is the Speakers' Corner,
To air your favourite grouses
Just send in that angry letter."

"Alright, Government, we see now
Freedom is real, not just baksheesh,
Please make the leash even longer,
But wait a sec! Why is it still a leash?"

Finally, I employed the quatrain to show that where there is no real freedom, both government and people suffer and also, at the same time, to plead, with vexed weariness, for change:

Singapore a fun city? Yes, of course,
Provided morals are not damaged.
Creativity in the schools? Oh sure,
Provided it's properly managed.

Freedom? Not too much of that
In case it gets out of hand:

So what if we end up as
The bland leading the bland?

❧

Singapore is the darling
In capitalism's embrace,
Maybe it's time to go for
Less flash and more grace.

Singapore is mega and supra
Technology's bright upstart,
Maybe it's time to go for
Less head and more heart.

So did the authorities respond to the versified criticism? No, probably for the following reasons:

1 They hadn't even seen it, since poetry in whatever form, would have no place in the PAP reading culture of purely serious, expository and argumentative prose.

2 Even if they had, they would have been a little flummoxed about a suitable mode of response. To reply to cheap, versified criticism with the usual serious official rebuttal would confer upon the criticism a dignity it certainly didn't deserve. On the other hand, to reply in kind using the same poetic form of quatrain would rob the rebuttal of the respect that was certainly its due.

Hence, the cheerful, playful little quatrain saved the day for me.

Ah, the Treachery of the English Language

A murderer was caught, not by the squad of trained detectives assigned to bring him to justice, but by English grammar.

The man had been a suspect in the murder of his wife who had gone missing. The detectives had sternly questioned him at various times, hoping that mounting pressure would cause him to make a slip in the story he had repeatedly told them about how she had gone missing. But the story stayed the same.

He said that his wife had gone shopping at the Prima supermarket at about ten in the morning, saying she would be back for lunch by one. She had called from Prima at about noon to say she would be a little late. He had waited till two, then had driven to the supermarket to do a search, and had ascertained, by talking to some of the sales assistants, that she had indeed been there. He called some of her close friends whom she might have visited after the shopping, but apparently none had seen her. Finally, in desperation, at about six in the evening, he decided to contact the police. His story was supported by alibis all the way.

He looked very distraught when some relatives came to comfort him and said tearfully, "She was such a good wife. She always took such good care of me. I will miss her badly."

Was such a good wife. *Took* good care.

He had used the Past Tense. But the wife had been reported to be only missing, not dead. It could only mean one thing: He knew she was dead. And that could only mean one thing: He had killed her. He had been betrayed by English grammar.

The Past Tense sets traps, not only for murderers, but also for liars.

There was a man who no longer loved his wife, but had to lie several times a day with the three affirming words 'I love you' because she demanded to hear them. She was one of those women for whom the ability to vocalise love was its very proof. The lying was very painful to him, for he was a very truthful man who couldn't bear to be guilty of the smallest falsehood. But he was also a peace-loving man, and the thought of upsetting his wife who loved him excessively was simply unbearable. He had to find a way out of the excruciatingly painful position. And, to his great relief, he did. He worked out a plan which he followed meticulously.

Whenever she exclaimed to him "I love you!", he reciprocated immediately with the same affirmation, with the same degree of enthusiasm, as she expected and desired. It pleased her immensely. She kept up this ritual throughout the day, so that their bedroom, the bathroom, the sitting room, the kitchen, indeed every part of the house, became love's echoing chamber. If she could have shouted out the words from the rooftop, she would have expected an instant response from him looking up from the ground. Such was her obsession. But he didn't mind at all, thanks to his masterplan.

Unknown to him, it was about to unravel. For suddenly the wife began to notice something very puzzling about his responses. They seemed to be made only under very precise, very odd circumstances, as if some force was directing them. For instance, he uttered "I love you" loudly in response to hers only when he was in the shower, but not when he stepped out to dry himself and get dressed. When he drove her to her mother's house on her daily visits there, he uttered them only when he was starting the car, but not once afterwards, during the long drive. At a party to celebrate her fortieth birthday, when she turned to him before cutting the cake and said cheerfully, in everyone's hearing, "I love you," he remained silent, much to her distress. But seconds later, amidst the loud cheering and clapping of hands after the cake-cutting, he said those three precious words, to her relief.

It was all so very mysterious to her! Why was he so inhibited at times, so forthcoming at others? Was something wrong with him, with her, with both of them?

She consulted a marriage counsellor who told her not to worry, as the fact that her husband responded at all after so many years of marriage was proof that he really loved her. She consulted a medical specialist who explained that it was likely a sign of the onset of male menopause. She consulted a behavioural psychologist who said it was probably some habit that had its roots in childhood. She consulted her church pastor who advised her that even if she suspected her husband was having an affair, she should forgive him.

She had the good sense to consult a linguist. The language expert explained that the matter had to do with English grammar. It was English grammar that her husband had had recourse to, in order to handle a terrible dilemma he had found himself in. The dilemma would have meant either telling a lie which would have been impossible for him to do, or upsetting his wife, which would have been just as impossible. But English grammar was in possession of a special feature that had enabled him, to his great relief, to get out of his quandary.

This helpful feature was the Past Tense form. It had enabled him to do simultaneously the two things he had thought impossible. That is, it had enabled him to tell his wife the truth, the hard truth that his love for her now belonged to the past: *I loved you then. I loved you when we first dated; I loved you for your sweet, soft, gentle voice; I loved you for your beautiful, sexy, slim figure.*

It had also, in the most marvellous way, enabled him, at the same time, to sound as if he were telling her what she wanted to hear. This was because the tiny *d* sound of the Past Tense of the verb 'love' could not be heard amid the loud sounds of falling water in the shower, of the car engine being started, of the laughter and cheering at the birthday party. So his wife heard only the Present Tense of 'I love you'. Our good man had been saved by verb inflection in the English language.

But clearly not from his wife's impending wrath, once the linguist had explained everything to her. Suddenly this language expert grew alarmed that the very expertise he had prided himself on, would be the cause of blame from an irate husband, if the wife should go on a rampage of fury, as she was likely to do. With a mounting sense of urgency to pre-empt the blame, he rushed to meet up secretly with the husband, and urged him to do the one thing that was sure to appease the wife: to say 'I love you!' clearly, unequivocally. One hundred times, if necessary. "I can't! I can't!" wailed the poor man. The Past Tense was his truth, and the Present Tense would be a lie.

The linguist had an idea. His expertise once again came to his rescue, but in a totally different way. This time, the solution had to do, not with English grammar, but with English pronunciation. He got the husband to practise saying, slowly and correctly, "Isle of Man, Isle of Wight, Isle of Yew", but in a special way, exactly as instructed. The anxious man had to repeat the names of the first two islands silently, in his head only, but when it came to the third island, he had to open his mouth wide and shout it out loud. "Isle of Yew!" *I love you!*

Needless to say, the wife was satisfied and the marriage was saved. The English language could be treacherous, but is ever forgiving of its users, and will tolerate the role of the expert linguist who is only too happy to help the hapless layman negotiate its many pitfalls.

I Am Liking Indian English!

Of the three major ethnic groups in Singapore, the Indians must be the most consistent, prolific and confident speakers of the English language. They are not necessarily more competent speakers than the Chinese or the Malays in their actual use of the language, or show a greater understanding of the rules of usage. Rather, this confidence seems to be the result of something much deeper, that is, race itself. It appears to be an inheritable trait of personality and character, going back through aeons, that is marked by extroversion, expansiveness, sociability and geniality that find natural expression in language, both spoken and written, taking it to amazing heights of eloquence. These qualities have never been part of Chinese conservatism or Malay reticence that is evident in their learning of a foreign language.

Take any equitable sample of Singaporeans who have been through English education in Singapore, and the chances are that the Indian speaker will stand out among his national counterparts. Whether in student clubs, college organisations, trade unions or political parties, Indian representation is disproportionately the greatest, their other ethnic colleagues seemingly contented to leave them to argue their cause, fight for their rights, create a lot of public noise on their behalf.

It is said that if you randomly throw a stone in the air where a group of Indians have gathered, it is sure to hit the head of a master of grandiloquence. It is also said that if four Indians gather to solve a problem, there will be at least five solutions.

Maybe it is envy of the Indian's linguistic versatility that has caused the others to associate it with all language-based vices: lying, flattery, exaggeration, insincerity, dishonesty, pomposity. But it is part of the expansive Indian character that they do not take any insult seriously or bristle at so-called politically incorrect statements, as the more sensitive Chinese and Malays would.

Many years ago, there was, in Singapore's political circles, a Chinese politician who thought to amuse his audience by telling them that he should not give a speech in the evening, for even if he had a large Indian audience, he wouldn't be able to see them in the darkness. The purely gratuitous reference to skin colour (which is typical of the obnoxious racist) had expectedly provoked some angry responses. But the hullabaloo was soon over, and never referred to again in the ensuing years. The Indian community seemed to have taken it all in their stride, moving past the small-mindedness of their Chinese detractor, to more important concerns in life.

I think Indians are wise enough to be less troubled by racism than by colorism, something completely different. Colorism is a preference among Indians themselves for lighter skin, as shown in the countless advertisements for skin-lightening creams, or the choice of the light-skinned Indian actress for the heroine's role in a movie. When the cause for division is internal, and the enemy is oneself, that division is much more difficult to heal, because it goes right to the core of the fundamental issues of individuality, identity and self-worth. Colorism could be even more disturbing if it is a stubborn leftover of British colonialism in India when the sahib and memsahib, white and pale, were continually shaded from the tropical sun and asked by bowing servants: "What will huzoor have?"

But overall, English-speaking Indians have long cast off the imperial yoke and have embraced the language as their own, cheerfully creating a new variety called Hinglish, which is a hybrid of Hindi and English. The postcolonial world is full of such new Englishes, including Singlish (Singapore English) and Taglish (Tagalog English). But if any offspring of the English language is likely to outlive the parent, it will probably be Hinglish.

There are many reasons for this. Firstly, the long history of British rule in India and the imposition of English as the official language throughout the vast subcontinent has meant that Indian speakers of English comprise the largest number of speakers outside Britain. Secondly, the long geographical arm of British colonialism reaching to virtually every part of the world, including Africa and Southeast Asia, subsequently creating a large diaspora of business-minded overseas Indians (over 16 million), has reinforced and increased the numbers. Lastly, the depoliticisation of English over time has meant that it will no longer be viewed with distrust as the language of the oppressors but will be accepted for its influence alone, whether in trade, technology or diplomacy. That of course means sheer number of speakers, of which Indian English will have no match.

But here's a small prediction. As India becomes increasingly prominent on the world stage and is courted by the big powers, including the US, Russia, China and Japan, she would very much, like the anxious bride wanting to look her best on her wedding day, wish to cast off all those aspects of her international image that are not exactly flattering. These would include the distinctive singsong Indian accent that often provokes mocking imitation, the tendency to use bombastic language to impress, the impossible tongue rolling, head waggling, and hand gesturing, that invariably make Indians a caricaturist's dream, the target of ridicule in comic films.

Witness the hilarity provoked by Peter Sellers' impersonation of the Indian in the movie, 'The Party'. Through a mistake, the bumbling Indian is invited to an all-whites party, but moves with complete ease among the guests, talking in a high-pitched tone, peppering his speech with extraneous exclamations ("Ooh, goodness gracious me"), offering deferential, almost obsequious salutations ("Indeed, sir, no indeed, sir") and grammatical oddities ("Especially I thought your song was very beautiful").

One of the best liked characters in the TV series, 'The Simpsons', is an Indian immigrant in the US who owns the Kwik-E-Mart. Apu is a most affable character, with a needlessly long surname obviously chosen to poke fun at Indian loquacity — Nahasapeemapetilon, which, whenever Apu introduces himself, he will be able to rattle off in a split second, but which non-Indians could never hope to memorise. He speaks with the stereotypical Indian accent, while rolling his eyes in a way that is quite inimitable. International Indian viewers of 'The Party' and 'The Simpsons' are broad-minded and large-hearted enough to laugh along with other viewers, instead of dashing off angry letters of complaint to the media.

It is precisely this expansiveness of the Indian character that has made Indian speakers of English most engagingly uninhibited, adventurous and creative. While other speakers are hesitant, fearing to make mistakes, the Indian speaker forges ahead, unabashedly indulging his love of all things lush and ornate and attention-grabbing in language use.

Thus he favours long, complex sentences with words heavy with formality and legal significance. It is said that the Supreme Court of India had once set aside a judgment on a decades-old rent dispute issued by the Himachal Pradesh High Court, as the judges needed time to understand the English in it. Part of it read thus: "The learned counsel appearing for the judgment debtor/petitioner herein submits qua the impugned pronouncement made by the learned Executive Court upon the apposite objections preferred heretofore by the JD/tenant manifesting therein qua the decree put to execution thereby not warranting recording of affirmative orders thereon….."

This is the worst that any legal jargon can descend to, but to its creator, it must be uplifting proof of true language mastery.

The Indian writer wants to write properly not only for important official documents but for equally important love letters. There is purportedly a book written by an Indian author giving suggestions on the right words to use when replying to a girlfriend's note: "Your lyrical missive has enveloped me in the sweet fragrance of our love." These instructional booklets must have been inspired by the *Kama Sutra*, their verbal contortions paralleling the marvellous callisthenics in that unmatched manual of love.

As if the English language is woefully inadequate for his needs, the Indian user of English liberally creates his own vocabulary: *freeship* (scholarship), *unmotorable* (referring to a road that is not suitable for use by motor vehicles), *upgradation* (upgrading of status or value), *prepone* (reschedule a meeting ahead of the intended time), *Eve-teasing* (teasing girls), *botheration* (great nuisance). Once when filling a form to indicate the number of members in his household, he reportedly wrote: "Four adults, six adultesses and six children." On another occasion, when he had to state the occupation of his father who was a garbage collector, he wrote: "Garbologist."

A major English novelist, E.M. Forster, put the Indian propensity for contorted grammar to brilliant satirical use in his novel, *Passage to India*. The climax in the novel is a court scene in which a young, troubled and confused English woman named Adela Quested has accused a young Indian doctor, Dr Aziz, of attempting to molest her in a cave. Her lawyer argues forcefully that brown-skinned males are invariably attracted to fair-skinned women, at which Dr Aziz's lawyer remarks softly but distinctly, "Even when the lady is so uglier than the gentleman?" The pronouncement reverberates through the courtroom, causing the Indian crowd to cheer and instantly drawing attention to the plain-looking Miss Quested and the handsome Dr Aziz. The peculiar Indian construction of the sentence highlights the contrast in the most startling way.

But my all-time favourite is a certain feature of speech unique to the Indian speaker. It is the use of the Present Continuous Tense to describe a habitual activity or a state of mind or a fact that would normally require the Present Tense: "I am getting up everyday at 6 am"; "I am having a lovely family"; "I am believing that we are ruled by destiny". In a light-hearted book I wrote about my experiences as a cruise lecturer on the *Queen Elizabeth 2*, I just had to include, with humorous intent, an Indian fellow traveller who woos me with the Present Continuous Tense all the way: "I am knowing that you are the right lady for me"; "I am desiring your company...", "I am wanting to know your feelings","I am fearing that I will miss you very much".

I wonder whether this misunderstanding of rules governing the use of English tenses, never seen in other non-native speakers of English, actually has to do with the Indians' special philosophy of joyous living? Indian literature is noted for its assiduous avoidance of tragedy and the graver issues of life. This is because, to the Indian, life is not one but many. Therefore what remains unfulfilled in this world is no cause for anxiety for it will be fulfilled in the next. Man is continually given opportunities to reach completion, to perfect himself. His flawed use of the Present Continuous Tense, provoking laughter from others, may actually be an enviable reflection of his lifelong optimism. Whatever the cause, it certainly endows his speech with an engaging spontaneity, candour and quaintness all its own.

I do declare: I am liking Indian English very much!

The Cinderella Story Thrice Retold

The fairy tale of Cinderella as told, grudgingly to her students, by a modernist, skeptical Singaporean teacher who believes that it is no longer culturally or socially relevant to Singaporean children.

Once upon a time, there was a beautiful young girl named Cinderella. She had a cruel stepmother and two stepsisters who ill-treated her and made her do all the housework. (Actually, this sort of situation would be unlikely in Singapore where ill treatment, whether of family members, maids or even animals, is not tolerated, and is punishable by law.) One day, a handsome young prince who was keen to get married decided to give a ball to which all eligible young women would be invited, for him to make his pick. (In today's democratic age, princes and princesses don't give balls to pick spouses. They behave like everybody else in the way they meet and marry their partners, sometimes encountering the most awkward problems that the tabloid gleefully reports. And they are not always handsome. You only have to look at Prince Charles and his wife Camilla Parker-Bowles.)

Cinderella of course was not allowed to go to the ball. But her kind fairy godmother came to her rescue, using a magic wand to turn her rags into the most beautiful gown, and a pumpkin into a beautiful coach to take her to the ball. (Of course all this is just fairy tale stuff which has nothing to do with real life. In Singapore, we are taught to solve our own problems, and not to depend on others, including fairy godmothers!)

But there was something that the fairy godmother told Cinderella to remember: She had to return home by midnight. Cinderella had a wonderful time at the ball, as the prince had instantly fallen in love with her. She was enjoying herself so much that she forgot the fairy godmother's warning. When the clock struck midnight, she panicked and ran off, leaving one of her glass slippers behind. The prince quickly picked up the slipper and the next day mounted a search for her. His men were to go all over the land with the slipper to look for the owner. They were sure to find her, for the slipper was so very small it would not fit anyone else. (Now this is the greatest nonsense of all. Any logical Singaporean will tell you that, given the great variety of foot sizes among women, no matter how small a slipper is, there will be at least a few women for whom it will be a perfect fit.)

And sure enough, Cinderella's foot slipped easily into the glass slipper. She was brought to the prince, they got married and lived happily ever after. ('Happily ever after' means 'up till the very end'. As you would know, very few couples today manage to do that. The divorce rate in Singapore is increasing; one in three marriages ends in divorce.)

The Cinderella story as told in Singlish.

Once upon a time, got a girl her name is Cinderlella. She very beautiful. She got stepmother and stepsisters who very cruel to Cinderlella, every day make her work hard do all housework no rest at all. Aiyoh! *Very* ker-sian *only. One day got a very handsome prince he want to marry a wife so he give a big party to choose wife. Cinderlella's stepmother and stepsisters they all go but don't allow Cinderlella so she stay at home very sad. Then her faily godmother help her she wave her magic wand and hey, hey, Cinderlella got very beautiful dress and she wave again and hey, hey, Cinderlella got pumpkin coach. Faily godmother she told Cinderlella must come home before clock strike midnight.*

So Cinderlella very happy to go to the ball. The prince he fall in love with Cinderlella because she so beautiful. She dance and dance very happy and forget about the clock at midnight. Then the clock strike and aiyoh! *Cinderlella she got very frighten and ran away. But she drop one glass slipper. The prince he pick up the slipper and he tell his men to go and look for owner. Sure to find her because glass slipper very small, can only fit Cinderlella's foot. And so Cinderlella she wear the glass slipper and she and the prince they marry and live happy ever after forever and ever.*

The Cinderella story as told by a psychologist trained in Freudian psychology.

The motif of the underdog who elicits immediate sympathy is strongest in the Cinderella tale, where an innocent, beautiful young girl suffers the cruelty of her stepmother and two stepsisters. The name of the protagonist, based on cinders or dying coal embers, evokes images of loss and death, emphasising the second half of the Freudian eros-thanatos duality. Cinderella must suffer loss and deprivation before she can enjoy the fullness of life and sexual fulfilment. Eros emerges from thanatos as soon as Cinderella's fairy godmother appears before her. With her magic wand which is clearly a phallic symbol, she transforms Cinderella's rags into a glittering ballgown, and a humble pumpkin into a magnificent coach, to enable Cinderella to go to a ball being given by a prince looking for a bride. But she gives Cinderella a warning: "Come home before midnight or else — ." The midnight hour in folklore is the witching hour, fraught with magic and mystery.

The prince instantly falls in love with Cinderella. She enjoys herself so much she forgets the fairy godmother's warning. Then the clock strikes, and she rushes away in a panic. The striking pendulum is another clear phallic symbol. In her hurry, Cinderella drops one of her glass slippers. The prince picks it up. The next day, he sends his men, with the glass slipper to go in search of its owner. The slipper is so small and dainty that it cannot fit anyone's foot except Cinderella's. The moment her small foot slips into the slipper in a perfect fit is a Freudian symbol of the act of perfect, final consummation.

Linguicide

The vast lexicon of the English language, including words borrowed or stolen from other languages over hundreds of years, may be compared to an antiques shop where there is a tiny corner dedicated to a special group of words that have to do with killing. All these words end with the Latin *-cide*. Beyond the familiar ones of homicide, genocide, suicide and infanticide, there is an impressive list of *-cides* to refer to the killing of figures of authority and power: regicide (of a king), dominicide (of a master), tyrannicide (of a tyrant), episcopicide (of a bishop). It is almost like a wish list.

There is also a plethora of *-cides* for the killing of family members: patricide and matricide (of the father and mother respectively), mariticide and uxoricide (of the husband and wife respectively), filicide (of children by their parents), fratricide and sororicide (of the brother and sister respectively).

Indeed, there are also *-cides* for the killing of members outside the immediate family: avunculicide (of an uncle), nepoticide (of a nephew), siblicide (of full or half siblings), senicide (of an elderly relative), fetucide (of an unborn child).

I confess to a fascination for these heavily Latinised terms securely ensconced in the English language, charged with portentous meaning. Like the idle browser in the antiques shop, I pick each one up gingerly, blow off the dust and ask: Why? Why this abundance of terms for familial killing when surely its opposite — terms for the protection of kin — would be more natural? The answer probably lies in their Latin origin. Latin was the language of a bygone era characterised by bloody dynastic conflicts, intrigues and conspiracies. One thinks immediately of kings and queens in the medieval ages who maintained power or ensured the desired succession by murdering all those who stood in the way, including their own flesh and blood, including even future threats not yet born.

I confess to a greater fascination for those *-cides* that refer, not to the killing of human beings, but the ideals espoused by them. This kind of killing is actually far worse, since ideals are supposed to outlive their human creators. I have found three of these most egregious *-cides*: famacide (the killing of reputation or honour), liberticide (the killing of freedom) and educaricide (the killing of creativity or the love of learning).

Once I was enjoying a leisurely stroll through the Botanic Gardens when I saw a mother and her small son stopping in front of one of the many signs that direct visitors to various places of interest in the garden. But it was, oddly, a sign placed in front of a large bin, which said 'Litter', that was getting their attention. The mother was pointing to the sign while speaking earnestly to her son and urging responses from him. When I heard the little boy repeat the word 'litter' several times, and then spell it out slowly, the first time looking at it, and the second time with his eyes closed, I realised that right in the middle of a beautiful garden where children were playing and laughing, a sad little boy was being grilled in English vocabulary and spelling by an overzealous parent. I had never felt more sorry for a child in my life. I could imagine his mother, wherever she went with him, pointing out words on signboards, advertisements, streets, buildings, and asking him to spell 'lift', 'fire alarm', 'sale', 'office', 'restaurant', etc. He would probably hate learning for the rest of his life. His mother had committed educaricide.

Then I realised that as an English language teacher in a secondary school, obsessed with teaching my students the rules of usage and burdening them with endless classroom exercises and written homework, I was well on my way to joining this killer parent. In our zeal we had destroyed what was far more important than any language skill: We had destroyed the love of learning, perhaps even the human spirit itself.

It was a moment of profound awareness and awakening for me. Suddenly I remembered one of my students, a shy, timid, hardworking girl named Puay Choo whom I was determined to help secure that all-important passing grade in the English exam paper in the GCE O-Level examination. I gave her extra coaching, and imposed extra homework, even though I was aware that she had to help out in her father's noodles stall in the market in the evenings. "All the more reason for her to pass the GCE, secure a good job and get out of the poverty," I thought with grim, self-righteous purpose.

Puay Choo barely passed the exam. I lost touch with

her soon after. When I next heard about her, some years later, it was that she had committed suicide. Apparently, she had been unable to cope any longer with her many family problems and had jumped from a block of high-rise flats near her home. My shock when I heard the news went beyond the expected consternation of a teacher tragically losing a former student. It involved a deep sense of guilt.

To what extent had I, in my uncompromising determination to make her learn the English language properly, failed to see her other, far more important, needs? How much did I know — or care — about her life outside the classroom? What brought even greater pain was this thought: Had poor Puay Choo been trying to tell me about her problems but was put off each time by yet another effort on my part to teach the correct use of the Present Perfect Tense, the correct use of the often confusing trio of 'take', 'bring' and 'fetch', the difference between the use of the comma and the semi-colon?

The experience was traumatic enough for me to want to do something about it. I knew the best thing to do was to write a story. Sometimes writers write stories for themselves, to save themselves. I wrote not one, but two stories, challenging my imagination to produce cautionary tales about young people *in extremis*, in the strongest possible language, with the most vivid images, so that once and for all, I would be shaken out of my delusions. I was my own teacher, mentor and healer.

In the first story, an English language teacher would complain incessantly to her colleagues about the mistakes that she was always correcting in the composition exercises of her students. "Look," she would say with a sigh. "I'm just so sick of their mistakes! Don't they ever learn?" She read out the offending errors from an exercise book. "Every day I have to help Father in his stall. He never satisfy always scold me I tell him I must do homework for Teacher but he don't care." The teacher gave a little groan.

She read from the exercise book again. "My father he drink and spend all his money on drink and sometimes he is drunk and beat my mother. Even when she sick, he wallop her." The teacher said gloomily, "It's that shy, mousy student Tan Ah Choo who looks almost ready to faint each time I ask her to answer a question. Imagine, she's going to sit for her O-Level in the next few months! I shall have to give her extra coaching lessons on Saturday. Oh God, how I wish I could help poor Ah Choo and the likes of her!" When the news reached the school, the teacher said sadly, "What? She jumped from the tenth floor? If only she had told me about her problems. But she was always too shy and timid to speak up."

In the second story, the same zealous English language teacher wanted to make sure that in the mid-term school exam, all her students would do well in her subject, and thus attest to her teaching ability. In particular she was determined that one of the students, also called Ah Choo, would do well enough to be streamed into Class A or B, rather than remain at the ignominious C. Ah Choo was a most likeable student, always attentive, enthusiastic, hardworking, never failing to turn up for the extra Saturday lessons that the teacher gave on her own time. Moreover, she was a very helpful student, always looking for opportunities to help the teacher carry her piles of exercise books, buy lunch for her from the school canteen during recess, run any errand. The teacher asked her worriedly, "Ah Choo, are you ready for the exam? Remember what I told you about the composition paper? Choose the right topic, don't write out of point. You know you've often done that." Ah Choo nodded her head and said politely, "Thank you, Teacher. I promise to try my best."

And indeed, a week later, Ah Choo did well enough to be promoted to A Class, to the teacher's delight. Ah Choo wrote a little note to express her gratitude.

Some days before the exam, the school caretaker had failed to report an incident, because he believed he had made a mistake, being unable to see clearly in the dim evening light. He thought he saw a young man climb through a window into the school staffroom, but when he went to investigate, there was no one. Besides, everything seemed in order, undisturbed.

What he hadn't known was that Ah Choo's brother, a bright engineering student at a polytechnic, had broken into the staffroom, hidden behind a cupboard when he heard the caretaker, then re-emerged as soon as the man had left, to break open the cupboard where, as Ah Choo had told him, the exam papers were kept. He searched for the English composition paper, which Ah Choo had told him would be in a blue file, found it quickly, memorised the four composition titles and left, unseen by the caretaker who was resting on his foldable canvas bed, enjoying the evening breeze. At home, Ah Choo's brother helped her all the way to prepare for her exam. Out of the four composition titles, he chose one that he could write about, easily and quickly. Meticulously, he wrote out the composition for his sister and helped her memorise it.

The English language teacher would often cite Ah Choo as the best example of the reward for all her years of dedicated teaching. She said, "Even after she left school, she would visit me, bringing me my favourite fruit, *laksa, mee siam*. She and her brother are in some business together. Big business. Apparently, they're doing very well and making tons of money!" Then one day the teacher read a news report about them being prosecuted by the law for corruption, including embezzlement. She said, in a shocked voice, "I can't believe this is happening to a former student of mine. She and her brother are going to jail! I will certainly visit her, to show my concern."

Suddenly, she became reflective, and said, "Come to think of it, there was something not quite right about Ah Choo even in those days. She told lies, and once tried to cheat a classmate of some money. But you know, she was so helpful and cheerful, she was the most enthusiastic student in my class, always wanting to speak better, write better, that I…" And the English language teacher's voice trailed off.

There is a *-cide* word — linguicide — for a teacher who is so single-minded in her passion to teach the correct use of the English language that she actually ends up killing it for those students struggling to cope with far greater concerns in their young lives. In the secret world of their painful family life, in the secret world of their own unruly ambitions, uncertainties and insecurities, they would surely have welcomed a teacher's alertness, understanding and guidance, unobstructed by any language teaching zeal.

English Wit at Its Best

Sir Winston Churchill is, without question, the best exponent of the use of the English language, the best exemplar of the language at its finest. His eloquence and oratorical power are without match. In 1940, in the war against the Nazis, he made three speeches to the House of Commons, which were so memorable in their use of rousing language, that they became known by phrases and sentences lifted directly out of them: the 'Blood, toil, tears and sweat' speech of 13 May; the 'We shall fight on the beaches' speech of 4 June; and the 'This was their finest hour' speech of 18 June.

It was as if anything less than this straight lifting out of the best lines from the speeches to form their titles would have been an insult to their sheer magnificence.

Of the three speeches, the one that seems to be the most quoted to reflect Sir Winston's finest oratorical moments is the 'We shall fight on the beaches' speech of 4 June. It has been endlessly analysed to emphasise the hypnotic effects of the repetition of 'We shall' and of the majestically sweeping invocation of the panorama forming the background for this determined will to fight the enemy:

'We shall fight on the seas and oceans, we shall fight with growing confidence and growing strength in the air ... we shall fight on the beaches, we shall fight on the landing grounds, we shall fight in the fields and in the streets, we shall fight in the hills, we shall never surrender.'

But even more than this mesmerising oratory, it is Sir Winston's playful wit, shown in the far less exalted settings of the cocktail party, the casual encounter, and even at home in his toilet, that has greatest appeal for me.

Once he was in an American city, as the guest of honour at a ceremony to honour him by setting up a splendid marble bust of him. During the ceremony, a beautiful, well-endowed blonde rushed in, breathlessly exclaiming, "Sir Winston, I've come for the unveiling of your bust!" Looking at her appreciatively, he replied, "Lady, I'd like to return the favour."

On another occasion, he was enjoying a drink at a party and getting a little tipsy. A large, aggressive-looking woman came up to him and said nastily, "Sir Winston, you're drunk!" He replied amiably, "Lady, I'm drunk and you're ugly. But tomorrow I'll be sober!"

Another drink-related episode has it that a concerned friend tried to convince Sir Winston that he was drinking to excess. "Am I?" Sir Winston responded cheerfully. "Well, shouldn't we all drink to excess?" And he raised his glass in a toast and said, "To excess!"

Sir Winston was adept at using the pun. Once, he was told about somebody whose name was Bossom. "How odd," he mused. "Neither the one thing nor the other."

But the classic example of Churchillian wit must be the occasion when he was in the toilet at home, and somebody came with the urgent message that the Lord of the Privy Seal needed to get some information immediately. Sir Winston replied coldly, "Tell his lordship that I'm sealed in my privy. Also tell his lordship that I can only deal with one shit at a time!"

The Delightful Limerick

One of the most delightful offerings of the English language is the limerick, a short five-line poem that is light-hearted in tone, and, in the hands of those brave enough, downright bawdy in content. My contributions are by comparison quite tame, but I hope that by the end of my experimentation with this most engaging form for testing the ribald imagination's limits, I will be bold enough to go the whole way of the limerick.

Currently, the limerick serves my purpose of wickedly depicting the world of a special group of men and women — the Romeos and coy virgins, the dirty old men, the nervous spinster and the artful gold digger, the anxious overweight woman and the bullying husband — for whom love and domestic bliss may not come too easily. My satirical purpose is neatly served by a favourite figure of speech that fits in well, the irreverent pun.

Both Romeo and the coy virgin come under the spotlight:

Says the virgin to Romeo, "O cease!
Head says 'No', Heart says 'Maybe' with unease;
It's worse than a dilemma,
It's becoming a trilemma,
For Below Heart is saying, 'Yes, please!'"

Says he, on his knees, "Ah, love is nigh!"
Says she, from her lips, a gentle sigh,
"Don't feel forsaken
My heart's been taken."
Says he, "But I wasn't aspiring that high!"

On the party guy and the daring girl:

A party guy who loves to mingle
Is often asked, "Are you single?"
Says he, "I'm swinging along
With wine, women and song,
I'm what you may call a swingle!"

A topless girl in church caused mayhem,
The priest said, "You must leave — ahem!"
Said she, "This is a slight!
I have a divine right!"
Said he, "Both are, but you must still cover them!"

On the dirty old man:

There was an old man who loved adventures
With young women he had bold ventures,
The older he got
The bolder each shot,
The last one was younger than his dentures!

A dirty old man who liked Shakespeare
Has renamed his play 'King Leer',
Dickens' 'Tale of Two Cities'
Is now 'A Sale of the Titties'
He's aspiring to be DOM of the Year!

On the hopeful spinster:

There was a spinster who stated,
"For marriage I'm surely not fated."
But on the very day
She went for an X-ray,
She gushed, "I've been ultra-violated!"

On the disgruntled overweight woman:

To be a top model and hit
One must be thin, dammit;
My scales and mirror
Expose the full horror,
I'm thick and tired of it!

On the bullying husband:

A woman from India made a vow
Never more to Hubby she'd bow,
Said she, "I'm a woman's libber!"
But he beat her and whipped her
And cruelly asked, "Who's sari now?"

The Language of Irony

I am sometimes asked which single writer has had the greatest influence on my writing, and I am hard put to give an answer, because there have been so many who, in one way or another, at some point or other in my life, have influenced me.

But there is one whom I name with some fond regard because, in a rather roundabout way, he has been responsible for a very important literary feature of my fiction — irony. It is irony of the situational kind, that is, where the story ends in the most unexpected way, with a complete reversal of situation.

This writer is O.Henry, the pseudonym for William Sydney Porter, an American short story writer who died in the early twentieth century. He became so famous for ending each story in the most surprising way, effecting a virtual turnaround, that his name has become synonymous with this special literary genre.

O.Henry's most famous story is 'The Gift of the Magi', in which a young, loving, married couple are in a dilemma because each wants to give the other the best Christmas present, but can't afford the expense. The wife wants to give her husband a platinum chain for his gold watch, which she has seen him secretly eyeing in a shop, and the husband wants to give his wife two expensive ornamental combs for her beautiful long hair. In the end, each, without the other's knowledge, finds the money. The wife secretly cuts off her rich knee-length tresses, sells it and with the money manages to buy the platinum watch chain. The husband also secretly sells his gold watch and with the money manages to buy the hair ornaments. The irony of course is that each of the gifts has now become completely useless for its intended recipient. But, as the title indicates, there is a second irony, a heartwarming one. Each gift may no longer have any use but because it was bought with so much love, it becomes the best gift of all, like the gold, frankincense and myrrh that the Magi brought to the Christ Child. Another classic O.Henry story, but this time, with a comical ending, is 'The Ransom of Red Chief'. Two small-time criminals kidnap the ten-year-old son of an important citizen, and send him a ransom note. But the criminals soon find they have every reason to regret their action. For the little boy is so energetic, noisy, playful and demanding that he wears them down. He plays a Red Indian Chief and forces them to play with him until they are totally exhausted. In desperation, they write another note to his father, offering to bring back the boy for a lower ransom. But the father refuses their offer; in fact, he says he will only take his son back if they pay him instead. In the end, the two criminals realise gloomily that the payout exactly matches the ransom that they were hoping to have.

I wish that, like O.Henry, I could use irony for heartwarming or humorous effect. The trouble is I seem to have a rather pessimistic view of the human condition, that makes my stories end with irony of the dark kind, a reversal of situation that is perturbing rather than moving or amusing. It hints at the working of some powerful malicious force out there that intervenes in human affairs, causing strange twists and turns that confuse or even destroy us. It may not be the extreme horror expressed in Shakespeare's *King Lear*, *'As flies to wanton boys are we to the gods/ They kill us for their sport'* — but it conveys a sense of desperation all the same.

I had already, alas, had that cynical view from a young age. As I looked around and observed events happening in the lives of family, relatives, neighbours, even total strangers, I had the tendency to seek out the negative rather than the positive aspects of these events, the conflicts and disillusionments rather than conciliation and fulfilment. My ever fertile imagination was quick to weave tales around these events, which invariably ended with dark irony, not the bright, cheerful kind of O.Henry's.

I remember a neighbour, a tradition-bound man who fretted over his wife's inability to give him a male child. Then at long last, after what to him was a disgusting succession of four daughters, he had a son. When I saw him giving the baby boy all the attention he never showed his daughters, a story immediately came into my head. It is exactly like the real tale, except that it includes an astonishing discovery made by the father as his son is growing up — the boy enjoys trying on his sisters' dresses and make-up. The father explodes in rage, kicks him out and never refers to him again.

There were more stories stirring in my head. I had heard my mother and her friends talk about a woman who lived down the street, whose husband, a completely devoted spouse, suddenly died. The wife was inconsolable. At his wake an unknown woman appeared, with three children. She said loudly to them, pointing to the open coffin: "Go and say goodbye to your father." My mother's story ended with the shock of the wife. But my imagination had already fleshed out a story with a distinctive ending. After watching the three children gather round her husband's coffin, the angry, betrayed wife rushes upstairs. There she changes her mourning garments of full black into a bright red dress and also applies bright make-up on her pale lips and cheeks. Then she returns to take her place beside the coffin downstairs, smiling and cheerfully greeting the shocked visitors, presenting the exact opposite image of the weeping widow of less than an hour ago.

There was a middle-aged man in our neighbourhood, a casual labourer, who had a hatred of Caucasians, the hated *ang mo kwee* or 'red-haired devils'. It was no secret in the little town of Kulim that the man's daughter was a prostitute in nearby Penang, supporting her mother and a brood of young siblings, as the man spent all his wages on drink. In my story, this daughter one day comes back on a visit home in a car driven by one of her clients. When the father sees that he is one of the detested *ang mo kwee*, he falls into a rage, especially when he is aware that there are people watching the Caucasian opening the car door for his daughter and saying something to her before driving off. As soon as he is gone, the outraged father unleashes his fury. He begins shouting at his daughter and is about to hit her when she says matter-of-factly, "He is my best client." Then just as nonchalantly she opens her handbag, takes out some money, and throws it on the table in front of the father. "Here's the money from him for your next round of drinking." The money lies on the table for a day or two, and then is surreptitiously picked up by the father. Making sure no one is looking at him, he puts it in his pocket, and goes out to get his next beer.

When I was only nine, I was fascinated by a very old man who lived down the street, in the care of his daughter-in-law, a seamstress whom my mother often visited. He was incredibly old, with long, scraggly white hair and beard that the daughter-in-law didn't bother to cut. He was kept in a small corner of the upstairs balcony, where he crouched, whimpering like a captive animal.

But what fascinated me even more than the old man, was a large coffin that had been bought for him, many years ago, now placed against the wall on the floor downstairs, and gathering dust. It had been bought by his children as a mark of filial piety. For, according to Chinese tradition, the worst manner of death was when there was no coffin for the body, such as death at sea. To assuage their old father's fears when he fell ill, his children had bought him the coffin, making sure that it was the old traditional kind with the massive curved edges that he preferred. But the old man continued to live for a very long time, even outliving two of his children.

Soon the coffin-in-waiting became a detested symbol of the stubborn persistence of old age. But there was an age-old belief that brought some hope. According to this belief, if knocking sounds were heard from the coffin in the middle of the night, that meant a death would take place very soon. The daughter-in-law and her family secretly hoped to hear these sounds, but none came. Year after year the old man kept his place in the corner of the balcony. The coffin gathered even more dust.

In my story, one night the sounds are indeed heard. But, unknown to the family, they have been caused by a mischievous young person in the house, who has actually gotten up from sleep, crept to the coffin and begun knocking its sides with a wooden bowl. The next morning, with high expectancy, the daughter-in-law goes to look at the old man, but he is still alive. The disappointment is just too much for her, and she thinks with increasing vexation, "I'll have to put him in the temple." The Temple of the Compassionate Goddess takes in destitutes abandoned by their families. Within a day of his removal from his place in the balcony, the old man dies. He is well over a hundred years old. The daughter-in-law tells her friends that just before his death, she heard knocking sounds on the coffin, and so was prepared for the old one's demise. She says one has to respect traditions that have been passed down from one's ancestors from time immemorial.

So there I was, with my tales a-stirring in my head ready to be given birth years later. As I got ready to write them down, I suddenly experienced a strange moment of awareness, indeed, it was a shuddering frisson. For the truth was that it was none other than the English language, ever my ally in my creative efforts, that had provided the very sentence structure which had inspired me to write my stories with their theme of irony. The sentence, inviting to be completed, was this: *The very … turned out to be … .*

Unconsciously and with ease, I had completed the sentence, each time:

The very male child he had yearned for after so many daughters turned out to be gay.

The very man she had been so devoted to turned out to be an adulterer and a traitor.

The very race that he despised and mocked turned out to be the greatest benefactor to his daughter and himself.

The very tradition of respect for the old that she had once shown towards her father-in-law turned out to be the cause of her final resentment against him.

The English language had actually handed me a formula, a useful shorthand, for my short stories! Which language could be so helpful to a writer?

I discovered, to my delight, that the formula could be applied at the highest level, to the narrative of world history and mythology itself.

The very apple that Adam and Eve believed would give them perfect knowledge and happiness turned out to be the cause for their expulsion from Eden.

The very disciple whom Jesus chose to be among his Twelve Apostles turned out to be the one who betrayed him.

The very device of the guillotine, designed to make death as painless as possible, turned out to be a symbol of the brutalities of the French Revolution.

The very oil that enriched the Middle East turned out to be the greatest cause of its instability.

The very cure for women's morning sickness during pregnancy — thalidomide — turned out to be the cause of miscarriages and deformed births.

Of course this formulaic sentence pattern could be used for happy outcomes of the O.Henry kind: *The very person he distrusted turned out to be a true friend. The very misfortune he had suffered turned out to be the greatest blessing.* But alas, I have once again to say that I envy O.Henry his optimistic and benign view of the world!

Of Goldilocks, Midas, Jezebel, Dr Pangloss and Many More

Many years ago, when I was doing an English Literature course in the University of Malaya, I had a classmate who spoke little, preferring to remain tight-lipped in the midst of animated chatter. But she liked to join in when the chatter turned to criticism of others, which she did with the most economical language: "He's a Romeo", "My uncle's a Scrooge", "She's Jezebel", "He has a Dr Jekyll-and-Mr Hyde personality". Each statement of course carried a whole load of unstated information about the subject.

I had enough knowledge of popular English literature to understand what she was saying, but just to make sure I fully understood the allusions, I would throw in the straightforward meanings by way of seeking confirmation: "Are you sure he's such a flirt?" "He can't be as stingy as an uncle I have!", "Tell me more about her scheming ways!" "You think there's something psychologically wrong with him?"

As long as this friend's allusions were from the Bible, popular myths or fairy tales, I had no problem: "He claims he has the Midas touch", "I think he's doing a

Pinocchio again", "I wouldn't go so far as to call him a Solomon", "Our David is going to meet his Goliath one of these days". But she became so enamoured of this figure of speech in the English language, that she came up with increasingly unfamiliar, even esoteric ones: "My sister's a real Pollyanna", "Did you hear what that Dr Pangloss said?", "It's a Sisyphean task that I would avoid at all costs", "If Singapore has a Quisling who deserves capital punishment, this guy's the one!" It didn't matter if her listeners looked nonplussed; indeed, that could have been the precise intention of someone who liked preening her fine linguistic feathers in public.

Wow. Pollyanna, Pangloss, Sisyphus, Quisling.

Well, if I was nonplussed, I didn't stop there. I wanted to know about these four characters whose names had become generic terms. I began to take a liking to the allusion because I could see its many advantages, both in speech and writing, for enthusiastic users of the English language like myself:

- The sheer economy of language when using the allusion makes it particularly useful for those occasions when one is not in the mood for talking too much. The allusion may be seen as a kind of shorthand in communication.
- The awareness of a shared understanding of the allusions being used gives a thrilling sense of camaraderie and conspiracy with one's interlocutors, as well as the rather juvenile, superior 'we know, but they don't' feeling.

- The awareness that one's repertoire of allusions can be endlessly expanded by simply delving into the inexhaustible riches of the English language is a delightful prospect for the lifelong learner.

I was quick to do research on the four allusions that had escaped me. It was certainly a pleasurable exercise, yielding not only interesting stories of the origins of these allusions but their broader metaphorical meaning.

A Dr Pangloss is an overly optimistic person, indeed to the point of being ridiculously out of touch with reality. He is a fictional character in a play by one of the most well-known satirists of the eighteenth century, Voltaire, who used the character of Pangloss to criticise the extravagant optimism of Leibnitz, one of the Enlightenment philosophers. Leibnitz had grandly pronounced that our world is "the best of all possible worlds", and that whatever happens in it (including devastating natural disasters) can only be "for the best". (I wondered what Dr Pangloss would have to say about World Wars I and II, the Holocaust, nuclear power?)

Pollyanna may be seen as the female counterpart of Dr Pangloss in being excessively, permanently cheerful. She is the central character in a children's book written in 1913, and her admirers see her in a positive psychological light, since she seems to be exhibiting a subconscious bias towards all that is positive, and a clear aversion of all that's negative. But her detractors (including myself) would describe a Pollyanna as an annoyingly naive girl.

Sisyphus is a character from Greek mythology, a king and sinner who is condemned for all eternity to what must be the most painful and meaningless task of all, that is, he has to roll a huge rock up a steep hill, watch it roll down and then roll it up again. He has to do this continuously, for all time. The Sisyphean task is a metaphor, in existentialist philosophy, of the pure absurdity of human existence, where, on the one hand, we yearn for order and meaning, and, on the other, find ourselves trapped in the formless chaos of the universe. Any allusion to Sisyphus can only create images of futility and despair.

While Pangloss, Pollyanna and Sisyphus are fictional or mythical characters, Quisling is a real one, whose name has come to be synonymous with 'traitor'. Vidkun Quisling was a Norwegian military officer and politician who shamefully collaborated with the Nazis during World War II. This surely would make him one of the most despised figures in history. It is possible that, in the future, he will be joined in the gallery of ignominy by his twenty-first century counterparts as well as by equally detestable figures such as Stalin, Idi Amin, Pol Pot and Saddam Hussein.

The one single character who is most alluded to in the English language comes not from history, fiction or mythology, but from a children's folk tale. She is Goldilocks, from the well-loved tale of a little girl who is lost in the woods but fortunately comes upon a house belonging to three bears who happen to be out. Now what distinguishes Goldilocks is her fastidiousness. She is tired but wants to sit only on the chair of the right size. Hence she rejects the chairs of Father Bear and Mother Bear as being too big and settles for that of Baby Bear which she has carefully tested to be just right. She is hungry, but of the three bowls of porridge on the table, only one is not too hot nor too cold for her. She is now sleepy and with the same fussiness, goes for the bed that is not too big nor too small. In short, Goldilocks goes for a Perfect Fit, nothing less.

In today's complex world, whether of science, technology, business or social interaction, where the search, invariably, is for the ideal balance between competing theories, policies and practices, Goldilocks' pursuit of the Perfect Fit must resonate very powerfully. The corollary is the Perfect Balance. There is the generally agreed ideal of what is known as the Goldilocks Zone, where every detail fully balances every other, producing an ordered, harmonious whole.

For instance, according to cosmological theory, the Earth belongs to this zone because it is the perfect distance from the Sun, and hence fit for living creatures. If it were too near, it would be too hot and waterless; if it were too far, it would too cold and frozen. Economic theory too states that to belong to the Goldilocks Zone, a country's economy must not be overheated, causing inflation nor too cold, causing a recession.

Indeed, because balance is invariably sought in every domain of human enterprise, the Goldilocks Principle can be universally applied, and has to be constantly monitored, in continually changing situations, to make adjustments. Means have always to be adjusted to ends; reality has to match ideals; ambitious goals have to be accommodated to available resources. It would be an interesting mental exercise to consider the major problems of today's world in terms of the Goldilocks

Principle, and see how the balance of compromise can be achieved between opposing forces. Some examples: the need to preserve press freedom, on the one hand, and the need to control an unruly, irresponsible social media on the other; the need to reduce income inequality vs the need to encourage capitalist entrepreneurship; the need to preserve the environment vs the need for continuing industrialisation.

Even at the personal and individual level, balance is crucial, for instance the ambitious young woman's dilemma about whether to put career before marriage, or whether to heed the warning of that direful 'biological clock'; the ambitious young politician's quandary about whether he is spending too much time in politics and thus neglecting his family. Reality dictates that the unavoidable final answer is equilibrium, symmetry, balance.

The opposing forces which need to be adjusted to each other to achieve this ultimate Big B may be neatly presented in a list: head and heart, reason and emotion, rationality and intuition, duty and pleasure, freedom and discipline, individuality and community, state control and private ownership, top-down dominance and bottom-up independence, religious authority and private conscience. The list could go on indefinitely.

The widespread acceptance of the concept of balance, so engagingly articulated in the Goldilocks Principle, will mean that the allusion to the cute little fairy tale character will never go out of use. No other character in real life or fiction comes even close to Goldilocks in her enduring power as a metaphor. But here's an intriguing thought. There is also universal acceptance of another concept: that of the fear of loss. It is human nature not to want to lose anything that makes life comfortable, such as financial security, job prospects, social regard, etc. Indeed, the fear of loss may be the strongest driving force of human behaviour.

Now there is a special word in Singapore for this fear of loss: *kiasuism*, a Hokkien term that literally means 'afraid to lose'. It can claim usage outside the country of its origin for it is now an entry in the dictionary of Australia's Macquarie University. The person who exemplifies this attitude is known as a *kiasu*, often a stock figure of fun in local literature.

Could the English language, at the international level, make an allusion to a *kiasu*, at some point in the future, with the same ease that it is now doing for a Scrooge, a Midas, a Hercules, a Casanova? Imagine conversations in, say, a university campus in London, in which the term routinely crops up, to refer to the not-exactly-likeable fellow student who regularly hogs the best seat in the lecture theatre, or the most recommended research textbook in the library. Imagine whispered conversations at cocktail parties in New York about the passenger on a cruise ship who makes sure he is the first at the buffet table to grab the most expensive stuff such as lobsters and oysters, well before the other guests come in. Imagine international newspapers with feature articles on human behaviour, alluding to the emergence of a certain trait of behaviour as observed everywhere in the advanced societies, for instance, in the tourist who loudly demands a discount on his purchases. Or the diner who meticulously goes through the bill at the end of the meal to make sure that he is not being overcharged. And throughout there will be allusions to the notorious *kiasu*.

Here's a little prediction. When that day comes, there will be some anxious Singaporeans who will feel obliged to make extensive use of the Internet to launch a robust defence of *kiasuism*, as failure to do so would mean a national loss of face.

The Cheeky Preposition

One of the secondary schools in Singapore that I had taught in, had this motto comprising two simple prepositions: Up and On. It was meant to be a rousing call to energetic effort and dedication to duty, accompanied by the jubilantly raised arm. But the creator of the motto had not reckoned with the possibility of another interpretation. It was an indecent one, shared privately to uproarious laughter, conveying a graphic picture of the physical preparation for the sex act, that is, the heaving of one body atop another. The indecency got worse with the addition of a third preposition to signify the completion of the act: Up, On and In.

The preposition — in, on, between, through, against, behind, beside, etc. — is arguably the naughtiest item in English grammar. Since its function is to show the physical, spatio-temporal relationship between two entities, it offers vast potential for salacious jokes and innuendos, especially when it employs the unfailingly irreverent pun.

Some examples:

A maidservant confides in a priest that the master had taken advantage of her.
Priest (horrified): "You mean he took you against your will?"
Maidservant: "No, against the doorpost."

Confucius says: Honorable man must not walk behind woman, or he will see her behind.

Riddle: How would you define 'mistress'?
Answer: It's something between a mister and his mattress.

The preposition 'for' can be equally cheeky, as seen in the following supposedly true incident:

Years ago, at the time when the beautiful movie star Elizabeth Taylor had achieved public notoriety by stealing Eddie Fisher, the husband of the popular actress Debbie Reynolds, the evangelist Billy Graham spoke to a large gathering. He said loudly, "We must remember that God loves even sinners. Therefore we must never condemn the sinner, only the sin. So let us all now kneel down and pray for Elizabeth Taylor." Someone at the back shouted, "It's no use. I've been praying for Elizabeth Taylor for three years now, and I haven't got her yet!"

Now here's a simple sentence containing the preposition 'for', which actually has four different meanings:

He went to market to get a pig for his wife.

(Before you go on to the meanings given below, you might want to try to work them out yourself.)

The four meanings:
1 He was sent on an errand by his wife to the market to get a pig.
2 He went to market to get a pig as a gift to his wife (she might not know about it).
3 He went to market to get a pig in exchange for his wife.
4 He went to market to get a pig to be his wife.

An Apology

Dear English Language,

I would like to apologise to you for the way even so-called competent users regularly misuse you, both in speech and writing.

I want to apologise for the use of *it's* in sentences such as 'The department has a policy to promote better use of it's facilities', 'This book examines the causes of war and it's terrible consequences.' I suspect that this error has become so common, nobody notices it anymore.

I want to apologise for this sentence which I picked up from an educational article on YouTube: 'My idea was for the audience and I to view a huge screen linked to my laptop.'

I want to apologise for a horrible semantic mistake made by the most widely circulated English language newspaper in Singapore when it reported, many years ago, a mass wedding to celebrate Valentine's Day. The heading for the report was: 'The bells tolled and tolled and tolled.' I couldn't believe what I read. 'Toll' is used only for bell ringing on sad occasions, such as funerals. It would have been bad enough for such a well-established, highly respected newspaper if the sentence had been 'The bells rang and rang and rang', since the English language provides the precise term 'peal' to describe the sounds of bells for happy, celebratory occasions. I wanted to write to the newspaper to point out their mistake, but changed my mind, in case they took offence.

I want to apologise for the Singaporeans' ingrained habit of using the question tag *is it?* indiscriminately for all sentence patterns: "You don't believe anything I say, is it?" "The opposition parties are going to stand for election in this constituency, is it?" "They have let you down again, is it?"

I want to apologise for incorrect sentences that have appeared in the written English even of university graduates in Singapore:

- The politician accidently revealed the true crime statistics.
- The Speakers' Corner attracted a large amount of people.
- We are not ready to discuss about the sensitive issue of race.
- The cost of the new gadget was very expensive.
- After declining for months, the manager decided on new ads to improve sales.
- The PR department sent my wife and I a written apology.
- Alot of the data could not be used.
- Increased unemployment will greatly effect the standard of living.

Although it's not my business, I want to apologise for the dreadful mistakes made by the former US president, George Bush. Here are some of the most notorious 'Bushisms':

- The goals of the country is to enhance prosperity and peace.
- They misunderestimated me.
- When we get the facts, we'll share it with the American people.
- I'm going to put people in my place, so when the history of this administration is written at last, there's an authoritarian voice saying exactly what happened.

I don't know whether I should apologise on behalf of those Singaporeans who, years ago, attended a certain function where the speaker was Prime Minister Lee Hsien Loong. During question and answer time, a member in the audience asked a question about a certain issue which the PM described as a 'no brainer', that is, something relatively simple, requiring no real effort to solve. But the audience was annoyed, thinking the PM was being insulting in implying that the questioner had no brains and was asking a most stupid question. The annoyance was great enough for the PM to offer an apology, most unnecessarily I thought. He should have simply explained what a 'no brainer' means (and perhaps referred the offended party to a dictionary or thesaurus).

I want to apologise on my own behalf for a mistake I made in an article some time ago, when I wrote about 'a myriad of problems', unaware that the preposition was redundant.

So, dear English Language, despite the fact that you are serving us so well, we often misuse, misunderstand and misrepresent you, subjecting you to all kinds of abuses. That's why we owe you a sincere apology.

Yours most apologetically,
Catherine Lim

Dear Catherine Lim,

Sorry, but you can't do anything about it.

I appreciate that you are a strong supporter and dedicated user, but if I had been continually mangled by no less than a native speaker, a frequent public speaker, the president of the most powerful country in the world who could have employed the best speech writer or copy editor, why do you need to apologise for Singaporeans? In any case, I am resilient enough to survive any degree of misuse. I will still be around, as strong and popular as ever, long after all of you, users and misusers alike, are gone.

Yours most victoriously,
The English Language

About the Author

CATHERINE LIM is internationally recognised as one of the leading figures in the world of Asian fiction. The prolific writer and commentator has penned more than 20 books in various genres — short stories, novels, reflective prose, poems and satirical pieces. Many of her works are studied in local and foreign schools and universities, and have been published in various languages in several countries.

Also by Catherine Lim

Fiction

Deadline for Love
The Howling Silence: Tales of the Dead and Their Return
A Leap of Love
The Catherine Lim Collection
The Bondmaid
The Teardrop Story Woman
Following the Wrong God Home
The Song of Silver Frond
Miss Seetoh in the World

Non-Fiction

Roll Out the Champagne, Singapore!
A Watershed Election: Singapore's GE 2011
An Equal Joy